PARIS FOR FOOD LOVERS

Elin Unnes

Hardie Grant

TRAVEL

Contents

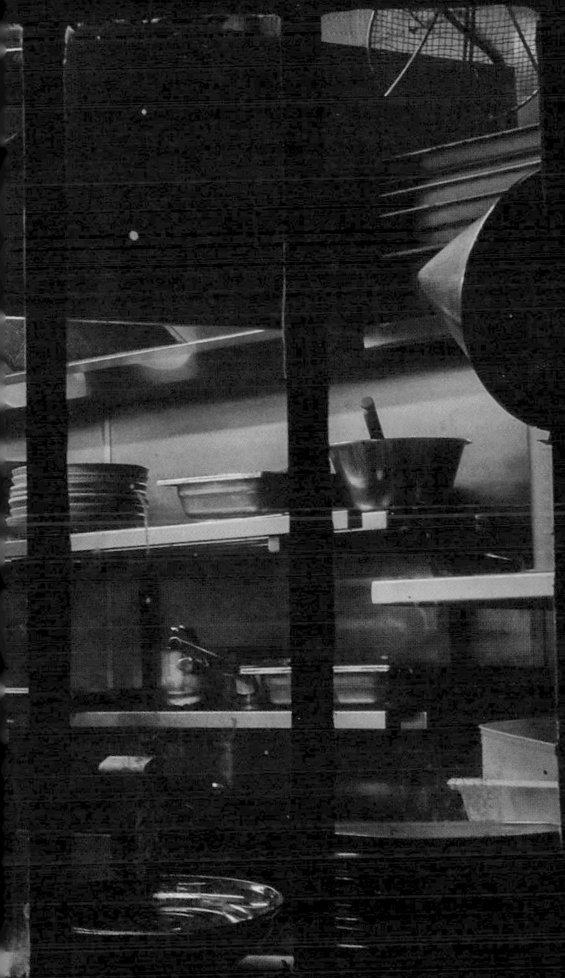

Legend

Ⓐ address
Ⓦ website
Ⓣ phone

🅱 bar
🆆🆂 wine shop
🆂 shop
ⓘ information
Ⓒ cafe
Ⓟ pizzeria
Ⓠ/Ⓐ question/answer
🆁 restaurant
🆃 tobacco shop
🆆🅱 wine bar
Ⓞ other

🐾🐾🐾 Crush Factor

Baratin, 6 April, 12.25am

Disclaimer

This is not a comprehensive guide. The contents only highlights the places where I like to eat and drink. I started just writing a guide for my Swedish friends who asked exactly that: where do you eat in Paris? For this reason, there are also some restrictions — for example, the fact that I seldom cross the Seine to eat. So this is primarily a guide to the Right Bank or, more specifically, to the 11th arrondissement. But that's as it should be. The 11th — *onzième* in French — is the best arrondissement in the world. It also happens to be where my husband, Stefan, and I spend the winter months of the year. And because we don't bring our holiday wallet with us to Paris, many of the restaurants we go to have reasonable prices. All of them can be described as vegetarian-friendly, unless otherwise noted. Generally, as long as you say you're vegetarian when you book a table, there are no problems.

The phrase "food lovers" on the cover is used to mean people who like to eat good food. And people who like to eat good food often enjoy other good things as well — for example, listening to good music and looking at pretty things. So I've included a bit of that too. This is a guide not only to food and drink, but to everything that makes Paris the capital of "the good life".

In this book, I often refer to my Swedish heritage and palate. So if you're not from Sweden, like me, I apologise if my personal tastes don't match up with yours. All I can say is that with my book you might still find some really good places to eat and drink, and my recommendations may still help you to make the most of your visit.

Finally, a suggestion: read this book with a pen in your hand, underline what you like, take notes in a notes app — this way the book becomes your very own little guide that travels with you, wherever you go.

Where are we going?

Alice B. Toklas, who moved to Paris in the early 1900s and became the partner of Gertrude Stein (the American novelist, playwright and poet), likened French cooks to the classic kings of Bourbon: "They learn nothing, they forget nothing".

But now, something has happened. Paris has a new type of cuisine. Again.

To me, the best description for what people have come to call "*nouvelle nouvelle cuisine*" is "*cuisine du marché*", or market-driven cuisine. The new French cooks are not necessarily French. They may be French-Japanese-Nordic or Fillipino or Australian. It doesn't really matter where they come from.

They listen to the same music (the good kind).

They're passionate about vegetables.

The restaurants where they cook serve handmade dishes and have mismatched chairs. There's tap water in unwashed old bottles, tattered posters on the walls and silverware barely licked clean between dishes. And there's nearly always a skilled sommelier pouring fantastic new organic and natural wines into the same old glasses.

It is an intoxicating, fabulous and wild world where menus change every evening, and where just about anything can happen. The new French kitchen proves that alchemy exists – for example, by serving a dish that seems to have materialized out of invisible spores in the atmosphere and found its way somehow onto your plate.

The one aspect of the new French dining scene that can seem a little elitist is that people are sometimes unwilling to give wine and food recommendations. "It makes no difference what is considered the best; people like what they like" is unhelpful advice if you have no idea what you like and couldn't name a French wine district to save yourself – at least, not until someone reminds you that Champagne is a place.

Au Passage

restaurant

🐾🐾🐾

In my mind, it all starts with Au Passage.

It was during winter when we finally decided to stop whining and do something, and that something was to spend the winter months on the Continent – that same year, Au Passage opened. When we first stepped off the night train at Gare de l'Est, with sleep-tousled hair and stomachs full of hot chocolate, I didn't know that the restaurant's owners, Audrey Jarry and Jean-Charles Buffet, had bought the old house in passage Saint-Sébastien. They had long dreamed of a certain kind of restaurant, one where it felt like you were eating at the home of a friend, and finally decided to open the place themselves. I didn't know any of this that night at Gare de l'Est. All I knew was how good it felt to go to Au Passage. In the midst

of happiness and new love in a new city, it felt completely natural – or beyond natural, more like a law of nature – for a place such as Au Passage to be there.

Peeking into the narrow alley between boring new buildings, you might at first think you took a wrong turn, but then you hear the Dead Kennedys' song *Too Drunk to Fuck* coming from the open window of the kitchen, and when at last you step inside the messy restaurant on the ground floor of an old, rickety building, it's like stepping into a new world – a world where someone has been eavesdropping on your food fantasies. From the start, it was all precisely as it should be: the portion sizes, the posters on the walls, the natural wines, the little shiso leaves beside every other plate. Actually, it was so perfect that I didn't think it was anything special. I didn't think it was anything other than how Paris usually is.

There have been many different cooks in the kitchen since my first visit, but Au Passage

continues to exist as a place of both anarchy and harmony in equal parts. The food is consistent, and the wine list is crammed with natural wines. One of the first chefs to run the kitchen was James Henry, and shortly after him Edward Delling-Williams. The Australian Shaun Kelly became a dad and moved on to cooking at the Australian embassy, where he also set up a kitchen garden on the roof. Peter Orr left for sister restaurant **Bar Martin** (p. 24) before opening his own gourmet tavern, **Robert**. For a while, the ambitious Swedish chef David Kjellstenius took over. At the time of writing, the Portuguese chef Luis-Miguel Taveres had taken over from Dave Harrison.

Regardless of who's in the kitchen, you always get the freshest, most flavorsome vegetables here. Imagine a bowl of fresh radishes, dipped in butter and shared by everyone around the table. This is even more decadent than it sounds, because more often than not the butter will be loaded up with oysters or something equally rich. The radish greens are so fresh and clean you can eat them too; they feel a little sticky on the tongue, but they taste bright and peppery. Mushroom toast also sounds simpler than it is: common pickled mushrooms mixed with larger fried mushrooms in a big pile atop a slice of fried, buttery sourdough bread swimming in broth, topped with what the menu describes as "walnut sprouts". These are not in fact walnut sprouts, but something that looks like beansprouts and tastes like walnut. (To this day, I'm still searching my seed catalogues to find this mystery crop.) If there is burrata on the menu, you must order it. The oysters are among the best in Paris. And I love the poster at the front of the room, which reads "The customer is king", with a picture of a guillotine.

For a while the pastry chef Quina Lon worked in the little kitchen, along with chefs Edward and Peter. At that time the kitchen was about the size of a handicap-accessible bathroom, and the bathroom, wall-to-wall, was the size of a broom closet. But Quina did things with dessert that would make the whore of Babylon blush. Once, during her time at Au Passage, we were stopped on our way out the door and sent back to our table. There stood several small bowls of ice-cream made with brown butter that left everyone at the table speechless. We didn't recover until we were outside in the alley with all its graffiti and precarious flower pots.

TIP

Dave Harrison, one of **Au Passage's** many chefs, likes to drink wine in the hip little restaurant **Chambre Noire**.

Ⓐ **82 rue de la Folie Méricourt, 75011 Paris**

These days Quina runs her own restaurant (p. 37), brown-butter ice-cream is all over the world and Au Passage has changed the way food is cooked and eaten all over Paris.

A few tips to make the most of your visit. First, it's best to go to Au Passage with someone you don't mind cosying up to at the table, so you can hear what they're saying

above the noise levels, especially later in the night. Second, the dishes are small and come out one at a time, so the smart move is to order as a group and share everything around the table. Otherwise, someone has to sit drooling over their mushroom toast as they politely wait for everyone else's plates to arrive. If you're here with colleagues or in-laws, it's wise to order two of everything – that way everyone has their own mushroom toast and their own potato fritter with algae. Everything is good, so you can't really go wrong. And if anyone is left unsatisfied, you can always order more.

If you're early (say 7pm or 7.30pm), slip into the bar for a glass of wine and some cheese before dinner, and everything's golden.

A 1 bis passage Saint-Sébastien, 75011 Paris
W restaurant-aupassage.fr
T +33 1 43 55 07 52

Q/A
Where do you eat?
Dave Harrison

Dave Harrison comes from Texas. He had barely turned 24 when he became head chef at Au Passage (p. 10). He was recruited through a long chain of relatives, mutual friends and an interview that basically went like this: "If you're still standing here in five days, you have the job". So Dave packed his suitcase and left Texas without so much as a backward glance. Dave had earlier worked at the celebrated restaurant Noma in Copenhagen, and at the time of writing he was back in Denmark, working at Copenhagen foodie-favorite Den Vandrette. He's cooking there while planning to open his own restaurant with some of his fellow Au Passage stars.

His style is more nose-to-tail than the typical market-driven cuisine – translated,

Do you have a signature dish?
Not really. Every time I think I'm on the way to creating one, I mostly want to ask it to go to hell, take it off the menu and try to come up with something new to get stuck on for a while.

What do you listen to while you work?
We listen to a super eclectic mix of different genres – metal, punk, disco, opera, Sade, Prince, techno. Right now it's mostly Nick Cave or The Birthday Party, New York Dolls, Happy Mondays, The Brian Jonestown Massacre, the Dead Boys … As loud as possible!

Do you have any favorite ingredients?
It's probably lemon juice or elderflower, or just whatever animal blood, innards, head or feet I have in front of me.

Do you have a regular restaurant in Paris?
If I'm going to be totally honest, I eat most often at **Best Tofu** (p. 78) in Belleville. Their soup with silken tofu, seaweed, mini shrimp and black vinegar is completely perfect and costs only 2 euro.

Where do you go to drink?
My favorite places to drink are **Chambre Noire**, **Le Grand Bain** and **Dame Jane** (p. 79).

What was the best dinner you've ever eaten in Paris?
The best meal I've had to date in Paris would be my birthday dinner at **Restaurant A.T**. It was multifaceted, surprising and generous. Plus Atsushi [Tanaka] is an angel. And he loves house music!

Do you have a simple but magical flavor combo, something you came up with yourself, inherited or have been served by someone else?
Lately I've been very into Champagne and super buttery, salty popcorn.

that means fewer bowls of radishes and more calf brains. Last time he cooked for us, Dave served, among other things, a sauce made of calf brains that the meat-lover in the group could not stop talking about, and about which the vegetarian in the group, who tasted the sauce, became noticeably quiet and thoughtful. At some point the words, "All this pig skin makes me sleepy", were uttered. All the dishes were so good that it seemed less like a dinner than a meditation, or like taking a short vacation from reality.

Jones
restaurant and bar

Paris is perhaps one of the world's most conservative places when it comes to cooking. But after 300 years of relatively slow cuisine development, nowadays things are moving fast. Only a few years after **Au Passage** (p. 10) opened, there were those who started to say that it was old news and they moved on, along with chef James Henry, to the even newer Bones. They were clearly wrong about Au Passage. But they were right about Bones. Bones has now changed its name to Jones, which among other things led to a fantastic example of clever graphic design: on the facade, the letter B was covered up with a white lightbox and a black letter J.

On the wine-spattered drinks list, a bit of tape barely covers the old letter B. And the place itself has gone from sounding meaty ("bone") to more universal (Jones is a very common surname), without ever becoming boring.

Jones also has one of Paris' most pleasing locations. Raw walls that look like they were hand-marbled by a drunken Egon Schiele, and lighting that doesn't prompt you to make an emergency call to your dermatologist. (Watt-love is popular in Paris.) The restaurant section is set on a raised floor, two steps above the open bar, so that diners can sit and gaze out at the street while eating.

At the time of writing, founder Florent Ciccoli was in the kitchen, and he served tapas, which I prefer over the more complicated regular menu that was served at Bones. I think the secret perhaps for Jones is that the hype around the restaurant built very quickly, which forced the kitchen to churn out dishes that are immediately likeable. The result is food that is traditional and delicious. That is the secret. That, and salt, which right now is perhaps Paris' least loved seasoning.

The portions are often small, but well thought through and easy to share (an important thing if you're out with people who tend to say, "No, you take the last bit!"). The dishes are simple but full of flavor: asparagus in lard (aka thin slices of fat); steamed mussels; a sophisticated burrata; roasted hazelnuts with broccoli; or the genius combination of grilled onion – halved and assembled so that each layer looks like a beached jellyfish – topped with a small mountain of creamy tahini, sprinkled with crispy buckwheat and pickled red onions. There will also probably be something acidic. There is almost always something acidic. But here they also serve a large, deep plate with a halved head of lettuce, which still drives me crazy because it's basically nothing more than grayish-brown cabbage in bouillon, but it's so good it curls the toes – like a Willy Wonka–cabbage, where every bite begins quietly roasted, then takes a detour through sauerkraut and finishes in caramelized, sweet-salty, umami-miso flavor.

If you forgot to book a table, slip into a seat at the bar. For a while there was a bar-only pork sandwich that people were very excited about. Both for the fact that a fine restaurant served a sandwich, and for the way it was served, which was spoken of as setting a new standard: a greasy baking dish containing a whole, fried suckling pig was placed directly on the bar, and for each new sandwich the nearest staff member piled a little of the meat onto a smooth bun, together with pickles or chili or horseradish or pickled radish or something similar. It's been a long time since I've seen pork sandwiches at Jones, but it still feels like a suitable example of what you can possibly expect at a bar seat here.

It was also at this bar that I learned the expression, "A glass is a bottle" (because we'd go through a bottle as easily as a glass, the wine was that good). The expression, while true for us, served no useful purpose except for France's biodynamic winemakers, whose bank accounts surely showed a measurable increase.

In the old days I would have recommended a bar-crawl that began around the corner, with a beer at **P'tit Bar** (p. 134), then continued with wine at Jones (partly since the beautiful, lavender-scented bathroom above the restaurant is a balm for the soul after a beer at P'tit Bar). Unfortunately you can't do that bar-crawl anymore, for reasons we'll come to later. It was on just such a bar-crawl that I lavender-soaped myself up so frenetically at (then) Bones that I lost my wedding ring without noticing. When later I ran, panic-stricken, back up the spiral staircase to the bathroom, I found the ring lying in the middle of the floor, in that particular way that lost wedding rings only ever do in Paris.

(A) 43 rue Godefroy Cavaignac, 75011 Paris
(W) jonescaferestaurant.com
(T) +33 9 80 75 32 08

"Clown Bar is
always fantastic ..."
(p. 32)

Q/A
Where do you eat?
Peter Orr

Peter Orr is from Adelaide in Australia, and began working as a busboy when he was 16. As a 19 year old, he put himself on a plane to London where he worked at Locanda Locatelli along with the world's first Michelin-starred Thai cook, David Thompson. Nowadays he lives in the 11th arrondissement in Paris, where among other things he is the chef at his own restaurant, Robert (32 Rue de la Fontaine au Roi, 75011 Paris), with its open kitchen, relaxed atmosphere and very sophisticated food. He also worked at Au Passage (p. 10) and Bar Martin (p. 24), and he flipped pancakes in the kitchen at Muscovado (p. 37).

Do you have a signature dish?
Maybe not a "signature dish" but pasta has become something people keep coming back for. We always offer at least one fresh, homemade pasta both at lunch and dinner. And when I was cooking at **Martin**, whenever I would put pig's head on the menu it would sell really well.

What do you listen to while you cook?
Mostly hip-hop. Action Bronson, A Tribe Called Quest, Chance the Rapper, that kind of thing.

Do you have any favorite ingredients?
Anything that's in season! But probably a perfect tomato is my favorite.

Do you have a regular restaurant?
Abri Soba (p. 99).

Where do you like to drink?
Any bar on rue du Faubourg-Saint-Denis.

When you tasted natural wine for the first time, where were you and what did you think?
I think I must have been at Brawn, a restaurant in London. If I'm going to be totally honest I did not love it at first. I am a big beer drinker, and the beer in London is so good. So it wasn't until I was here in Paris that I got the taste for natural wine.

Where was the best dinner you've eaten in Paris?
Clown Bar (p. 32) is always fantastic, but the best ever has to be at **Saturne** (p. 93).

Do you have a simple but magical flavor combo, something that you came up with yourself, inherited or have been served by someone else?
I have cooked Thai food for a few years, and I have definitely taught myself a few interesting combinations inspired by that cuisine. I use sugar in my savory dishes, and salt in sweet dishes. It is a direct result of having been exposed to Thai cooking.

Bar Martin
restaurant and wine bar

Bar Martin is a restaurant and wine bar that was started by former employees of **Au Passage** (p. 10) with help from their old employer (the same thing has now happened so many times that Au Passage seems like an octopus with edible arms – a new tentacle sprouts with each young chef who grows up in this kitchen and then starts their own). Over the winter holidays there are big baskets of oysters on the terrace for 1 euro each, along with bottles filled with colorful oyster knives. Inside, people eat small plates and drink natural wine at messy tables.

It was here that I learned the French word *fusillade*, or shooting. We had ordered a lot of small delicacies, as you should here, and I had just stuffed myself with a very good fried Camembert when a brusque waiter suddenly gave us the bill and said that it was time to go. I thought perhaps that he was going off-duty – it happens sometimes, with French waiters, and then they must close the cash register. And I thought that maybe, exactly like everything else in Paris, you must already know this in order to understand what's going on. But Anders, our dining companion who has lived a long time in Paris, asked what was wrong and the waiter answered, "Fusillade."

It was the night of the Bataclan theater massacre in 2015, but this was before the information showed up on all the major news channels. There weren't even any police on the street yet. Afterwards Stefan and I talked about how Bar Martin must have had a call from Au Passage, which sat only one street away from the Bataclan theater. People must

have crammed into the restaurant, in the midst of the chaos. But I have never ventured to ask about that night.

We actually should have been heading home a few weeks earlier. Instead we decided to stay. We had spent several months in Paris, and many hours in Bar Martin that night, with doors locked and lights dimmed, tucked way inside the building along with the staff, who continued to pour wine, and all of the other guests, who immediately lit one hundred cigarettes.

(A) **24 boulevard du Temple, 75011 Paris**
(W) **bar-martin.fr**
(T) **+33 1 43 57 82 37**

R WB 11 arr

Aux Deux Amis

restaurant and wine bar

Aux Deux Amis is a little wine bar serving tapas and a lot of natural wine. "A lot" is perhaps the wrong phrase: there are only six natural wines served per day here – three white, three red, plus maybe a bubbly and/or a cider. Each morning the new wines are written by hand on a mirror in front of the bar (never mind if the handwriting is illegible, it's all good). But since they don't serve anything other than natural wine at Aux Deux Amis, percentage-wise it still seems fair to say it's a lot of natural wine.

The bar lies in the middle of rue Oberkampf – a long hill that people have trudged up hunting for fun since at least the '90s. Probably longer. For about as long, it's been said that Oberkampf is passé, but never mind that. Oberkampf is a great starting point when you're out wandering aimlessly in the 11th arrondissement. I say this even though I usually try to avoid the street around midnight because things can degenerate into student chaos.

Out front of Aux Deux Amis stand two long wooden tables that are often full, even when it's below freezing outside. Inside, the venue is crowded with small tables – the place is so little that the whole restaurant is visible from the street. It's open all day, for both lunch and dinner. This is ambitious in any case, but just

as often the door is inexplicably locked. On top of that, the place can become very messy towards the end of the day, particularly because many of the staff seem to work themselves into a frenzy (on a recent night I saw two waiters do a football-style chest-bump maneuver). I'm relieved every time I get a table with a waitress here.

Anyway. The food justifies everything. The food, and the fact that you don't need to book a table. I usually show up early (around 6pm) and have a little glass of wine and a couple of slices of manchego cheese that is served with the ultimate accompaniment, membrillo. (Membrillo is a firm, sweet and glutinous fruit paste made of quince.) The salty, fatty cheese and the caramelized fruit are a perfect snack before a late dinner. But it also happens that I often decide that the wine is so good, and the membrillo so delicious, that I'll stay at the bar and order several small plates, or even everything on the menu, and let snacks be my dinner – like a single tortilla, alone on a saucer, lovely, moist and full of potatoes (I can't even think about the pandemonium that broke out when I said the wrong thing and was served a frittata instead). After the tortilla is served, I might have a large piece of creamy mozzarella drenched in mild olive oil, with a pinch of black pepper on top. A few simple snails, swimming in a thick, flavorsome gravy (I have seen a tranquil French child whining for this dish, in order to pop the snails into his mouth one by one, looking like he was eating candy). There are often small bowls filled with things that seem like a rich fisherman's leftovers: shellfish, warm cooked potatoes, a few bits of leek, maybe a little mustard, some herbs and a mass of other unidentifiable but delicious

things. If I were you, I would finish with a little glass of calvados to put hair on your chest.

You can turn up later in the evening also, around 8pm on a Friday, if you're adventurous and have been keeping up with your zen exercises. The trick then is to step in cautiously but decisively. Try to make eye contact with a waiter or waitress who seems to have their wits about them and point toward a table. When that's done, steal one or two (at most) centimeters at the counter. Order as much soft, light natural Italian wine as seems manageable and wait for a table. And then just try to remember that all living creatures are closely connected in some way, just not always as closely or literally connected as during the second seating on a Friday night at Aux Deux Amis.

Et voilà, all is well.

Ⓐ 45 rue Oberkampf, 75011 Paris
Ⓣ +33 1 58 30 38 13

R B 11 arr

Clown Bar
restaurant and bar

Nearly everyone in Paris has their panties in a twist over Clown Bar. The only problem is that the personnel at times have been so epically unpleasant that it was difficult to go here (and note that this opinion comes from someone whose favorite wine cave is run by a wine dictator). One visit to Clown Bar used to mean rigorous preparation. It was best to stick to the following checklist:

1. Be arrogant.

2. Dress to impress (the only person I know who always received good service is a stylist for French *Vogue*).

3. Start by ordering an extremely serious, expensive wine.

We still continued to go to Clown Bar, mostly because they serve proper Italian espresso. And pretty quickly we developed a sort of trick to keep the price of coffee down: your rump shouldn't, in any way, touch any of the chairs. Not even the barstools. Hanging your ass in the air means the coffee costs 3 euro, while contact with the seat raises the price to 6 euro (possibly more, given the type of price increases mentioned on page 88).

But then … something happened. Clown Bar became pleasant. Now it's easy to book a table, to speak French and English and probably a couple of other languages (both the waitstaff and the kitchen staff are from a little bit of everywhere). And to have a coffee without looking like you swallowed a fire poker.

The food is still a dream. In the same sense that James Joyce is a writer's writer, Clown Bar is a chef's kitchen – and a little more

digestible than Joyce. One winter my friends Kocken and Konstnären ate dinner at Clown Bar and left there completely destroyed – and not just because the waiters kept pouring wine long after they stopped ordering (Clown Bar still delights in people who delight in good natural wine). Among the golden lamps shaped like palms, framed by tiled walls covered in paintings of drunk and evil clowns, they were served dishes that were so special and so good that they didn't understand how they could possibly return to their normal lives. Calf brains, pork tacos, a pair of doves, a fluffy mini pie filled with goose liver and a little piece of duck, after that, beef tartare, after that, … things got a little blurry, explained Konstnären, because it seems it's a long way to the water tap at Clown Bar.

On the menu, brains came before the starters, under the title "pastimes". They aren't served as a sauce, or as a little seasoning on top of something else, which nearly all the good places did that winter. It was just a brain, exactly as you'd imagine it would look, on a plate with chopped scallions and ginger on top, lying in a hazy pool of tosazu sauce. This type of decadence is of course what professional eaters crave, and that's exactly what the chef is. For me personally, it's enough with the giant oysters swimming in silken Jerusalem artichoke soup, and mussels served just as they are but still better than ever before. You can eat good vegetarian food here too, but you have to say so when you book a table.

The only thing about Clown Bar that still makes me do involuntary pelvic floor exercises is the price: a lunch plate costs 38 euro. And sometimes they do things like offering new potatoes in March (16 euro for a small plate), which I always think is sort of philistine.

The late sitting on a Sunday is fun: you don't have to abandon your table halfway through the night (standard for many places with two sittings), but can hang out with your bottle of wine. Since Clown Bar is open Sundays, unlike many other good restaurants, the place is filled with all the cooks whose restaurants are closed.

(A) 114 rue Amelot, 75011 Paris
(W) clown-bar-paris.com
(T) +33 1 43 55 87 35

TIP

Clown Bar's owner also runs the restaurant **Saturne** (p. 93), where everything is incredibly, unbelievably, super super good and expensive.

⊙ 11 arr

Muscovado
cafe
🐾🐾🐾

Quina Lon is the pastry chef who used to make the show-stopping desserts at **Au Passage** (p. 10). In the teeny tiny kitchen she created dishes that were so innovative that the other kitchen staff often thought here desserts were actually better than the main course, which must be as close to a Nobel Prize as a pastry chef can come. Now Quina has her own place, Muscovado, which she runs with her sister Francine.

Two good things about Muscovado are that they serve breakfast all day, which is pretty unique in Paris, and that they stay open on Mondays, which is shockingly unusual. They also always serve a small cake (more like a cookie) and a soft cake (say, carrot cake). But things are never really as simple as they seem at Muscovado, and even if you order something as basic as American pancakes, the plate always includes so much more: over two fat but simple pancakes lies something that looks like a small, melting scoop of ice-cream; then on top of the "ice-cream" ball are two bits of banana, and the cut sides of the banana bits are caramelized like a crème brûlée. A quick visual inspection of the pancake and topping tells you instantly that this dish will require some rationing. The trick is to get the two delicious things on top (the "ice-cream" and banana bits) to last long enough that they reach the bottom pancake. But then you take a little test bite and realize that the pancake itself is so rich and delicious that it is perfectly fine to eat plain. A slightly greedier test bite tells you that

rationing isn't going to be necessary. Between and under the pancakes are little surprises, like an advent calendar for the mouth, and you turn up more and more caramelized bananas, little islets of banana mash, and ... cheese? Why has no one mentioned that you can have melted cheese on pancakes?!

And what at first looked like a small ice-cream scoop is clearly not ice-cream (which is actually an irritating topping on warm dishes, because first it cools down and then melts and soaks into what's under it). These scoops aren't actually cold, but room temperature, and so beyond delicious that just licking the knife is enough for the whole brain's flavor center to drown in the unmistakeable taste of sweet, browned butter and extra thick whipped cream.

It can also go like this sometimes. You have a bit of a slow morning, after having been out late, drinking a lot of red wine at **Aux Deux Amis** (p. 28). You venture out for a coffee, to see if that helps. You go to Muscovado, because you haven't yet decided whether you should have a bit of cake or not, but you are certainly not prepared to rule out the possibility of cake. The air is cold and damp, and you have to hold your coat closed with one hand, but it doesn't matter because it's warmer than it has been for several weeks. The cafe is empty, but a young man with dark, bushy hair sits on the terrace. "Hello hello", he says when you arrive. Inside the bar, Quina stands preparing lunch. The day's soft cake turns out to contain large amounts of cocoa, grated beets and root beer, which settles the question of cake. You sit at an outdoor table and while you wait for the coffee and cake, a well-dressed, slightly timeworn older man wanders by: hand-knitted cravat, three-piece suit that looks like it also might function as pajamas, house slippers for shoes, and a large, empty shopping bag in one hand, so old that all the printed ads on it have worn off. "Hello Hello", says the young guy at the outdoor table to the old man, who stops to chat. "What do you do?" asks the old man. "Cook? That's a good job. You speak French well also, exactly like the woman inside. Where does she come from? … Philippines? You don't say. Well, bye now, I must hurry along." Quina comes out with the coffee and cake, and the young guy says to her, "He loves you", and nods towards the old man. Quina smiles, blushes and disappears back inside. "He walks past here two times a day, so she usually gives him a bit of cake or some vegetables to take home", the guy says, in Australian-English. "She is a fantastic baker. We've worked

BROWN-BUTTER ICE CREAM
by Quina Lon

5 oz (150 g) butter
3 egg yolks
1 oz (25 g) corn syrup
   (glucose syrup)
22 fl oz (650 ml) milk
4 oz (100 g) superfine sugar
1–2 teaspoons sea salt
ice-cream machine

Brown the butter in a saucepan. Mix the egg yolks and corn syrup in a bowl. Slowly warm the milk in a separate saucepan over medium heat – do not boil the milk. In another saucepan caramelize the sugar to a dark amber colour, or to approx. 240 degrees F (120 degrees C). Remove the milk from the heat and pour it, in two batches, into the caramelized sugar. When the sugar and milk are fully combined, add a little of the sugar-milk to the egg yolks mixture, to stabilize the temperature. Then pour both mixtures into a saucepan and heat to 185 degrees F (85 degrees C). Remove from the heat and add the melted brown butter (which should still be melted) and the salt. With an electric hand blender blitz until the mixture is smooth like a cream. Place the cream in the refrigerator to cool, then run the cream in the ice-cream machine until it's ready.**

Serve the ice-cream with a pinch of sea salt on top, to bring out the nutty flavor of the brown butter.

** I have only made this ice-cream in a Pacojet kitchen appliance, so I can't guarantee how it will turn out in an ordinary ice-cream machine.

together before. I'm here now to help in the kitchen." So you ask the young guy: you haven't possibly, at one point, happened to have set up a kitchen garden on the roof of the Australian embassy in Paris? The young guy takes the question better than most would. "That wasn't me", he answers. "That was Shaun Kelly. He is a fierce dude. He worked as a restaurant chef, but had a little kid. He needed to change his lifestyle. So now he cooks for the Australian embassy."

You smile and take a bite of your cake, which is coal-black and indescribably moist, with a thick layer of fresh, sweet, pure white cream cheese on top. You eat every crumb of the cake, because it also seems to cure hangovers. Then you head out, waving goodbye to the young guy, who you now understand is Peter Orr, and who is still sitting and smiling and greeting passersby. Then you go home and correct a section of text that just this morning said, "XXX had a little problem with his visa and now cooks at the Australian embassy, where he also set up a kitchen garden on the roof." You delete a comment that said, "Can it have been Peter Orr? Double-check". And now you may have a glass of wine with lunch, because you've worked so hard and done such meticulous, important research all morning.

It can be like that sometimes. In Paris.

Ⓐ 1 rue Sedaine, 75011 Paris
Ⓣ +33 1 77 16 31 32

Q/A
Where do you eat?
Quina Lon

Quina Lon is from Davao City, Philippines. She lives in the 11th arrondissement in Paris, and worked at Dinner by Heston in London before starting as pastry chef at Au Passage (p. 10). Now she runs Muscovado (p. 37) along with her sister. There she cooks fine food disguised as casual American comfort food.

Do you have a signature dish?
At Muscovado it has to be *pain perdu* (French toast) with a topping consisting of homemade *spéculoos* (a gingerbread-like cookie), bananas, brown-butter crumble and whipped brown butter.

What do you listen to while working?
When I'm running the kitchen, before the cafe opens, I like to listen to Little Dragon, Alt-J, Rhye or James Blake.

Do you have any favorite ingredients?
I love vanilla in desserts. It is a perfect complement to everything. In savoury dishes there must be bacon. Smoky, salty, fat. It's the ultimate comfort food.

Do you have a regular restaurant?
If I dine out it's usually Asian, so **Deux Fois Plus de Piment** (p. 52) or **Abri Soba** (p. 99).

Where do you go to drink?
Most often to **Bar Martin** (p. 24). Or **Mary Celeste**, if I want to drink cocktails.

When you tasted natural wine for the first time, where were you and what did you think?
It must have been a bottle of white that we had at **Saturne** (p. 93), with lunch, around four years ago. It was light and a little funky, but in a nice way. I remember that it worked well with the sorrel sorbet we had for dessert.

What is the best dinner you've eaten in Paris?
A three-course dinner at **Frenchie**, when it was a little easier to get a seat, and Gregory Marchand was actually in the kitchen and cooking food, like seven years ago! I was only visiting in Paris, and if I am really honest I didn't have particularly high expectations. It turned out to be a very special meal.

I also appreciated the way the sommelier skilfully matched the wine with each dish. With the desserts we had an exquisite glass of Canadian ice-wine and it was gorgeous.

Do you have a simple but magical flavor combo, something you came up with yourself, inherited or have been served by someone else?
Clearly coconut flower meringue* – it gets very "savoury" and umami-ish, and dark in color. But also calamansi curd** and sesame and ginger crumble.

* Coconut flower meringue isn't a meringue that tastes like coconut, but a meringue made of sugar that comes from the coconut-palm flower, with natural flavors of caramel.

Where do you eat?
Francine Lon

When Quina Lon stopped working at Dinner by Heston, a two-star Michelin tavern with a kitchen consisting of 50 cooks, her little sister Francine Lon had just started working there. Francine is also a baker, trained in New York, and after having had enough of working 18-hour days, she followed her sister to Paris' 11th arrondissement, where the two opened Muscovado (p. 37) together. For my birthday once, I ordered a cake from Muscovado with instructions that it should also work as a cocktail, with rose liqueur as a base. Francine baked a very exotic thing with pistachio nuts and lemon, and since then, this flavor combination of pistachio, lemon and roses has etched itself into my brain like a dream I never want to wake up from.

Do you have a signature dish?
I don't have a special signature dish, but I like to make layer cakes with interesting flavor combinations, like banana and chocolate chip cake with passionfruit and *dulce de leche****.

What do you listen to while working?
In the cafe we usually play soul classics, but if there's no one else there I blast Drake or Robyn on Spotify!

** Regular lemon curd is made of lemon, butter, egg and sugar. Quina replaces the traditional lemon with hybrid calamansi, a tart fruit that used to be defined as a citrus and has recently changed its Latin name to *citrofortunella*. In most of the world it's grown as an ornamental plant, but in the Philippines they use both the fruit and the leaves, from which you can extract a delicate oil that is believed to mitigate symptoms of anxiety and depression. Another *citrofortunella* that shows up often on our plates in Paris lately is the limequat, a hybrid of lime and kumquat.

*** Make your own *dulce de leche* by placing an unopened bottle of sweetened condensed milk to simmer in a water bath for two hours.

Do you have any favorite ingredients?
Eggs! They are the most versatile and incredible ingredient ever!

Do you have a regular restaurant?
Bar Martin (p. 24).

Where do you go to drink?
If I'm not already drinking at Bar Martin, then it's **Mary Celeste**.

What is the best meal you've eaten in Paris?
It would have to be a three-course lunch at **Saturne** (p. 93) in 2014. I was just in Paris to visit then.

Do you have a simple but magical flavor combo, something you came up with yourself, inherited or have been served by someone else?
I love French fries and vanilla ice-cream. I like to dip the fries in the ice-cream.

Orientation

Paris is shaped like a snail. Some say Paris is shaped like a cinnamon bun, but I believe all Parisians, including the ones who decided Paris should look like a snail, would protest until hoarse if they heard that. (One of the things Parisians love most, after snails, is to protest until hoarse.)

The first time you stand in Paris with a map in your hand and someone says, "Paris is shaped like a snail", it sounds like nonsense. Someone comes over, peeks at the map, does a swirling motion and says, "Look, exactly like a snail". After a while it's like when someone shows you a moonscape-looking photo of their not-yet-born child: "Look, there's the foot!" You nod and smile.

Then, when you've been in Paris a week, you're all, "My God, it IS a snail!" Before you see the snail it's invisible, and once you see it, you can't unsee it. I don't know how it happens, I don't know when it changes. I won't even try to explain the snail. The thing is to accept it.

The snail is brilliant.

First, the snail is brilliant because it has a namesake pastry (the *escargot*) that ensures there's a line down the street outside the bakery **Du Pain et Des Idées**. On weekends weeping tourists stand and photograph the facade of the bakery because Du Pain et Des Idées, shockingly enough, is closed then*, and everyone who waited until Sunday to buy their snail pastry must go without.

Secondly, the snail is brilliant because each section of its shell has a number. The sections are called *arrondissements*. The numbers go from 1 to 20, and these numbers correspond

with the two last digits in the postcode for each address in Paris. This makes it easy to read the address of a place and know how far away it is, even if you've never heard of the street.

* I personally avoid Du Pain et Des Idées. Not because there's a line out into the street – that's true of all the good bakeries in Paris – but because it always seems to take an eternity to order. It's chock-full of intellectual Americans who are so ashamed of

where they're from that they whisper in English when they order and the staff must constantly ask three times to hear what they say. But nobody seems ashamed enough to just learn how to say "une baguette" and "un escargot".

Getting around

You can walk nearly everywhere in Paris. The city consists partly of old villages merged together, and the village mentality lives on. There's also nearly always a good bakery, a good wine bar, a good farmers market and a good lunch restaurant in every area. "Like, seven minutes" is the standard answer when someone wants you to come and meet them for a glass of wine and you ask how far away they are.

There are loaner bicycles if you want to move a little. The bicycles are cheap, the city's hills are concentrated in certain areas and the traffic isn't as scary as it sounds. Look for "Velib" signs to find instructions. The only thing you have to know about Velib bicycles is that it's strictly forbidden to keep a bicycle out late at night. Then all of the bicycle stations are full and you have to cycle around for ages, usually desperate to pee, to find a place where you can leave your bicycle. As a rule, the journey ends further away than where you first picked up the bike.

The metro never seems to connect just the stations I want to go between, but overall it's easy to navigate. There are automatic ticket machines at each station; they speak English and the cheapest alternative is to buy a packet of 10 tickets at a time. The same ticket works city-wide, but doesn't include transfers – once you've left the metro or bus, you'll need to stamp a new ticket.

Taxis are notoriously difficult to flag down, and you can't call for one in Paris. The surest way to find an available cab is to go to a taxi rank. People who work in the Latin Quarter usually know where the nearest taxi rank is. An important detail is that Parisian taxi drivers don't like to take four passengers. The front seat is reserved for a thermos, empty croissant packet, water bottle, declaration papers and an MP3-player with a cracked screen.

Getting lost is nothing to be ashamed of. Paris is not like New York or Barcelona, where the roads look like a grid of chicken wire laid over the city. Instead, in the 1800s one of the city fathers decided it would be much snazzier if Paris streets radiated out, like stars, from various important places. This meant that all of the wide boulevards, which look straight, in fact slant off in totally the wrong direction, to someplace you don't want to go at all. It also makes it impossible to get around just by your sense of direction.

Asking for directions is basically a way of socializing. Just as in old TV game shows, you have to ask the question correctly to get the right answer: always begin with "*Bonjour*", wait for a response, then continue with "Do you know this neighborhood?" Then, all that's left is to go there.

Bar-crawl on the hill

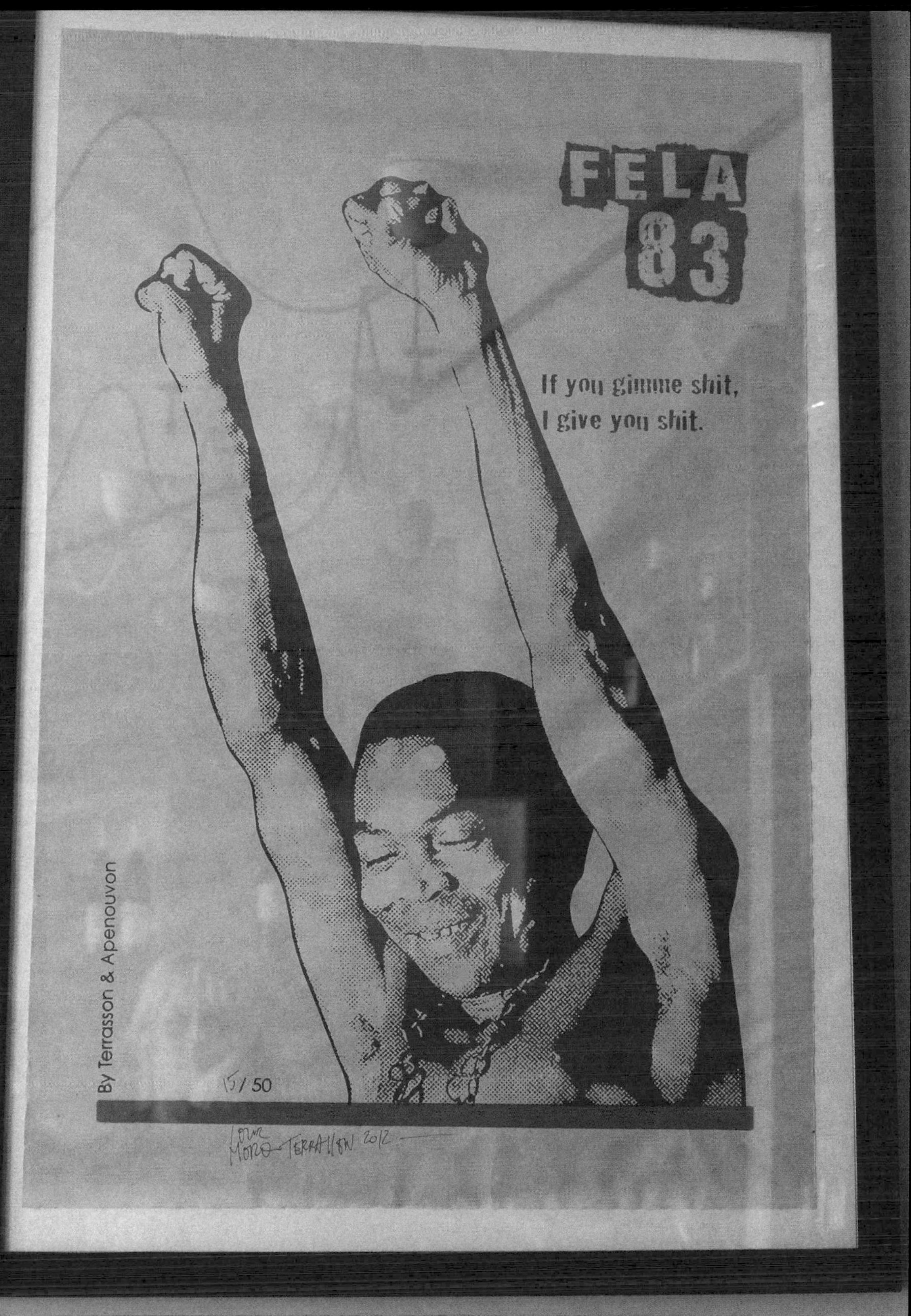
FELA
83
If you gimme shit,
I give you shit.
By Terrasson & Apenouvon
15/50

Ordering wine

Some people bring along a French phrasebook on a trip. Or maybe a translation app. Maybe you've studied a little French as a tween. Maybe you are confident that "*vin rouge*" is a thing you can still order in French; or maybe "*bière*", because it kind of sounds like "beer", and obviously beer is the same thing in any language. Go for it! Order in French. But know this: French waiters have follow-up questions about as simple as anything on CNN. It's like they've taken a course in some kind of cognitive interview technique designed to make it impossible to lie. Do you want a bottle, carafe or glass? Which size of glass, small or large? Should the wine be heavy or light? Where should it come from? Would you like it chilled or at room temperature? And so on, and so on.

The easiest thing is to order based on a region; instead of saying "*vin rouge*" say the name of a region. It doesn't even really matter what you like, just say "Côtes du Rhône". They always have Côtes du Rhône wine and it's often the cheapest, almost like a house red. Furthermore, a small glass of cold, tart Côtes du Rhône never tasted so good as at a chilly outdoor table in Paris.

Ordering beer

Beer is never just beer, either. In Sweden I can get irritated when people make it a thing to order a "*stor stark*" ("big strong", aka a pint of strong beer), because a "*stor stark*" doesn't just mean a "*stor stark*". It means "I don't care, give me the cheapest, most generic beer you have". But in Paris it's different. A bartender tells me that if a guy comes into his bar and orders "a beer" it can mean anything. A beer? Oh, you mean a *demi blanche Picon* (a half-pint of wheat beer with a shot of a sickly green southern-French bitter mixed in). Of course, one "beer", coming up! The thing that comes closest to a regular old beer is a half-liter of light lager, which in French is called a "*pinte de blonde*". If you don't specify "blonde", the bartender will immediately ask, "Blonde, white or brown?" when you order your pint. There is a delightful size under a pint also; "*demi*", literally a half pint. This is the best size for afternoon drinking. Frenchmen can nurse a *demi* for hours. There are two other sizes also. "*Galopin*" is a half half-pint. This is what Ernest Hemingway's kids used to order when they were out together. Smaller than a *galopin*, there's the very obscure size "*fœtus*" (fe-tuss), which is a half half half-pint, and not much more than a splash to rinse the bottom of a glass. Only order a *fœtus* from bartenders you know.

R 11 arr

Deux Fois Plus de Piment

restaurant

Not far from **Au Passage** (p. 10) lies this little Sichuan restaurant (the name means roughly "twice as spicy"). The place is something between a hole-in-the-wall and a shoebox, but as soon as they open (around 6.30pm for the dinner service) it's possible to sneak in without having booked a table. As early as 7pm the place begins to fill up with spiffy-looking youths on dates, neighbors who don't feel like cooking dinner, food-industry types – those who crave that particular throat-tickling, spicy Sichuan flavor. This is a good place to start from, before going out for a climb up the beer-drenched hillside of rue Oberkampf. Especially because rue Oberkampf can cause you to forget why food is important, and then, the next day, you're reminded of this in a very unkind way.

At Deux Fois Plus de Piment both French and Mandarin are spoken, and you pay with cash. The dishes are steaming hot, by turns sticky and salty-sweet, piquant and peppery, saucy and nutty: spiced cabbage, broccoli with garlic and an exciting chopped eggplant. Many plates are spiced with those super fun Sichuan peppercorns. If you happen to bite into a peppercorn, your mouth turns a new color, which then colors every bite you take thereafter.

All the dishes are available in different heat levels: you choose the strength when you order. I always forget what heat level I usually get, and last time we were there I had the following conversation with yet another of the stern-faced waitresses you meet in Paris:

Her: How hot would you like the dish?
Me: What levels are there?
Her: One to five.
Me: Ok, medium?
Her: *Blank look, frustrated blink*
Me: Sorry, three. I'll take three.
Her: Three is hot. Very, very hot. Very. Hot.
Me: Sorry, which levels did you say there were again?
Her: One to five.
Me: Ok, two then.
Her: You'll get one.

One is like a normal, medium heat. Two is so hot that I can't even imagine how hot three is. I still don't even know if four and five even really exist, or if it's just a linguistic confusion.

There are vegetarian dishes on the menu, but it's good to emphasize that the person eating them is a vegetarian, otherwise some meat might accidentally show up in the dish.

A 33 rue Saint-Sébastien, 75011 Paris
T +33 1 58 30 99 35

B 11 arr

Rush Bar

bar

Almost directly across the street from **Deux Fois Plus de Piment** (p. 52) is this pleasant pub that you must always call Rush Bar, never just Rush, or else no one will know what you mean. The wooden floors are beautifully timeworn and the atmosphere is so warm that you hardly notice that a window has been broken for years. The pub is run by a British expat, and the whole bar is very English. Just like many other Parisian places, Rush Bar pretends to be nonchalant about its drinks but the young French bartenders will read you the riot act if you so much as suggest that Absolut is a good vodka.

People come here from all over the neighborhood to have a nice cup of tea or a proper British pint, to check out the extremely violent rugby matches on TV or to drink a quiet glass of wine on the terrace. There's free internet and, at times, an excellent lunch is served. According to British tradition you order at the bar, which always leads to confused Frenchmen sitting at tables and then shouting their orders to even more frustrated young French bartenders. At the time of writing Rush Bar didn't officially serve food, but it's nearly always possible to have a small packet of vinegar potato chips with your beer. If they're out of potato chips, you can buy your own packet from the convenience store down the street.

One time when a dove, in the French manner, crapped on my head, I ran in a panic into Rush Bar's restroom where I stuck my head under the tap without thinking about the fact that you can't dry long hair with toilet paper. The realization came when I stood doubled over with long wet hair hanging into the sink. I peered up between the wet strands, saw that a plugged-in hair dryer was hanging over the sink and nearly started to cry at this thoughtfulness.

There's also an interesting photo collage inside the ladies' bathroom. My favorite is

a picture of Kris Kristofferson without a shirt, from the film *A Star Is Born*, where Barbra Streisand, with an ecstatic expression, appears to be listening intently to his bowel movements.

Ⓐ 32 rue Saint-Sébastien, 75011 Paris
Ⓣ +33 1 43 57 32 04

Ⓑ 11 arr

Le Zéro Zéro
bar

This place is more commonly known as Double Zero, or "The Double" for short, and there isn't really much to say about it other than that it's open late, you should have peed before you got here and they use a smart system where 1 euro from each guest's drink is donated to the DJ (so don't be alarmed if your first order is more expensive than the stated prices). I always feel like Lennie in *Of Mice and Men* here: all the drinks, even cocktails, are served in pliant plastic glasses that you have to hold very delicately so as not to crush them.

Loud techno with too much treble and really young Frenchwomen are the norm, but once you get used to it, there are few places that can satisfy your drinking needs as well as The Double.

Ⓐ 89 rue Amelot, 75011 Paris

B 11 arr

Nun's Café

bar

As many of the older venues close down on rue Oberkampf, and more of the traditional rock dives disappear, you have to look more carefully for bars that don't smell freshly painted. Thankfully, the old world is alive and well at Nun's Café, which lies just alongside Oberkampf. The music is well chosen, prices are low, installation of the window seals is careless, the furniture is exactly the same and the toilets are an adventure. It was also here that I, late one night, met a young Lebanese artist-in-residence-scholarship consultant. He told me that he'd lived all over the world, had experienced famine and exile, but the hardest thing he'd ever done was to try to find social connections in France. It's lucky that there are still bars where you can talk with strangers without there being anything strange about it.

A 112 Rue Saint-Maur, 75011 Paris
T +33 6 30 46 92 13

B 11 arr

UFO Bar

bar

UFO is a tremendously reliable bar when it comes to playing rock music. However, it is

Order a mojito at your
own risk at UFO Bar

a tremendously unreliable bar when it comes to which type of rock is played: everything from Danzig's greatest hits to Mayhem's most discordant live album (which, to the untrained ear, sounds like Venom doing a cover of a tumble-dryer full of gravel).

The cracked vinyl sofas and the hand-written signs make UFO look like a dive bar, but if you order a cocktail it is always meticulously crafted – this is the kind of place where bartenders go to drink. For myself, I'm usually too impatient to handle waiting for a cocktail, but if I want one I usually take one of their shaken shots: they explode on the tongue like tiny flavor-crystals and give the same kick as a normal shot, but are sufficiently diluted so that you don't have to go home as soon as you've had one.

Stay in the room where the bar is, and avoid the "lounge". In the lounge outside you'll find hordes of French students and a small, broken, graffitied restroom with a sign that says writing graffiti will get your hands cut off. And French students have an almost superhuman ability to turn the most unwelcoming places into "cute" sitting rooms.

In the basement, people dance, dance, dance to Tarantino-style music, which is always fun.

A 49 rue Jean-Pierre Timbaud, 75011 Paris
T +33 6 09 81 93 59

bitter French coffee. As per French tradition, we have had food poisoning here at least once, so maybe it's best to stick with just drinks.

Charbon is only closed a few hours a day, but the later it gets, the more expensive it becomes to drink here, so keep checking the prices if you're on a tight budget.

A 109 rue Oberkampf, 75011 Paris
W lecafecharbon.fr
T +33 1 43 57 55 13

B R 11 arr

Café Charbon
bar and restaurant

If you can't find a place with cracked vinyl sofas, graffiti and hard rockers – or if those places haven't opened – Café Charbon on rue Oberkampf is perfect.

When you're in Paris, it's as if Café Charbon has hand-picked exactly everything that's nice about the city – the decadent charm, the unwillingness to rust, the beauty that comes with genuine wear and tear inherited from generations who refused to be practical and instead focus on pleasure.

Sit at an outdoor table and drink a small glass of cold, tart red wine, regardless of what temperature it is outside (in Paris you never freeze). Or sit at the bar surrounded by the large, old mirrors and drink small cups of

Drinking coffee

A cup of coffee is called *café* in French. A small coffee with warm milk is called a *noisette* (noa-sett) and a large coffee with warm milk is called a *café crème*. Espresso with warm water, which is called an Americano in the rest of the world, is called *allongé* (alon-jé). But my suggestion is to let the *allongé* coffee be; don't drag out that espresso, but rip it off like a bandaid on a hairy arm.

In the 1600s, when Frenchmen started drinking coffee, they imported the beans from Arabia. When it became clear that coffee wasn't a temporary fad, people began to grow coffee on the French Antilles (the seven French colonies in the West Indies) instead, to avoid giving money to foreigners (in France the colonies aren't called colonies but, as in the post, "*outre mer*" (overseas): the land mass is still French to them, it's only the ocean around it that's changed).

The Italians make their coffee from a different bean to the French, who chose their coffee varieties based on which plants thrived in their colonies, where it tends to be a little cooler than the rest of the world's coffee plantations. That's why French coffee is so bitter. This could also explain why the French still hold onto the wartime-favorite chickory coffee: coffee blended with the roasted and ground roots of the weed-like chicory plant.

Le P'tit Garage

bar

●●●

This is (my husband) Stefan's absolute favorite bar. They have a really good happy hour: a pint costs 3 euro between 6pm and 8pm, Monday to Saturday and all Sunday. This is good to know because many places in Paris aren't ashamed to ask 11 euro for a pint, even if their Côtes du Rhône wine costs only 3 euro.

On Thursdays, an old skinhead used to stand in the bar and open oysters until his hands bled. A dozen cost 10 euro and it turned out that oysters go amazingly well with a light lager.

The best room is the one just to the left inside the door, and the best table is the oblong school bench by the window – the distance from the loudspeakers is perfect and you have a good view of the street, where ladies in cleaning uniforms walk sweet dogs, and young guys smoke cone-shaped, hand-rolled cigarettes in cars with rolled-up windows, while skinny guys chew on sunflower seeds and argue about the tip.

The walls are graffiti-wrecked and the music they play is almost exclusively garage rock. But on certain enchanted afternoons it happens that Moro – the cute, shy little guy in a sailor's cap – plays a classic Rossini album on the old record player behind the bar. Because it's on a record player you can hear the whole album, which is fun in these days of infinite playlists and Spotify-mania. Recently Moro, the skinhead and the oysters had disappeared from the bar, and the record player had an old PC for company, but Le P'tit Garage is still better than most of the other rock bars.

It's best to get here early – as the night progresses, French students fill the place. I would like to say that the toilet is one of Paris' shabbiest, but unfortunately I can't say that – there are worse toilets in Paris. It doesn't happen that often, but if someone has fallen asleep in the ladies' room, just say so at the bar and they'll fix it.

If you pass by here during the day, before the bar has opened, you can glance into the carport just beside Le P'tit Garage. There you can still catch a glimpse of Moro where he stands and tinkers with an antique car in the place that gave the bar its name: it still functions as a workshop for bartenders and regulars. And beware the chicken that lives in the garage. This workshop also confuses people who try to meet us at Le P'tit Garage, as they go to the wrong place, just before the little garage, where a prominent sign shows the word "Garage". Le P'tit Garage is under the sign that says "*Boucherie*" (butchery).

A 63 rue Jean-Pierre Timbaud, 75011 Paris
T +33 6 16 01 48 15

Oysters as poor-man's food

In the 19th century there were Portuguese port towns where only the poorest fishermen ate oysters. Their oysters were large and meaty and thrown on the grill, where they opened and then boiled in their own sea salt.

The amount of oysters called for in old recipes – and that some French people still use – also says something about what an affordable food oysters must have been. French friends tell of relatives who would eat 10–20 oysters themselves with no problem. Jean Anthelme Brillat-Savarin (the French epicurean and gastronome) had a friend who used to eat 32 dozen oysters. As a starter. My favorite grower, the Norwegian Annemarta Borgen, wrote in *Min Fiskkokbok* (*My Fish Cookbook*) that oysters have always been cheap food for the people. Before the North was converted to Christianity the uncivilized Scandinavians were mad for oysters. She also tells of Charles Dickens' comedic series from the 1800s, *The Pickwick Papers*, where impoverished Sam Weller complains about all the oysters he has to eat: "Poverty and oysters always seem to go together". Another favorite is Samuel Johnson, the British lexicographer and celebrity (at least in lexicographers' terms). Despite literary successes he remained uniquely, epically poor for nearly his entire life. But he always paid for a daily ration of 12 oysters – for his cat. The author Gertrude Stein, who was known to eat lamb injected with cognac for lunch, modified her diet when she left France on a tour of the USA; before her lectures she would simply eat only honeydew melon and raw oysters.

In Paris, where food is expensive, it always feels like a kind of sport to look for cheap, good oysters. One trick is the markets. They move around the city depending on the day of the week – this way no street is disturbed more than one or two days a week. But they are never further away than what an elderly, penniless lady can dramatically drag herself to. If you show up early, there are always cheap goodies. You can find the market address by googling *marché + arrondissement*.

To my mind there's another reason oysters are a poor-man's food: the additional ingredients required, i.e. nothing at all. Possibly a quarter squeeze of a lemon slice. Or, if it's really a party, a half-piece of coarse bread with nothing on it. Once, at a restaurant in Sweden, I had oysters served with a peppermill and the reason was that's how you eat them in Sweden: with freshly ground black pepper. After that I ate oysters with black pepper for half a year – there's some kind of chemical reaction between the pepper and the saltwater, which makes the oysters taste even saltier. Even when I went to Paris the first time, I ordered pepper with my oysters at **Au Passage** (p. 10) and the waitress dragged herself away to search for the restaurant's only peppermill. She handed it over with a sideways smile, as if I'd ordered ketchup. I am pretty sure that was the first and only time anyone had ordered oysters with pepper in Paris, but I like it so much that I still eat them this way sometimes. But maybe not at Au Passage, because it feels a bit like asking for Tabasco sauce (which thankfully you can ask for at **Clamato** (p. 110) because they have a fantastic homemade Tabasco and there's no shame in it).

Oysters are rich in magnesium, but just like everything that is rich in magnesium, you destroy the mineral if you combine it with what it goes best with, which in the case of oysters is Champagne. However, oysters are also the perfect breakfast the day after you have overindulged in oysters and Champagne: magnesium eases cramps and soothes anxiety. These days I always save a pair of oysters for breakfast.

The size is another contradictory thing about oysters. Oyster sizes are given in numbers from 0 to 0.5, where the largest oysters, counterintuitively, are 0. I struggled for many years to remember this (why is it so hard to remember: "It is how I think it is, but the opposite"?). I finally learned a way to remember it, after I saw a poster in a restaurant in the Norman twin cities Deauville–Trouville. (The cities are large and are separated by a stream, but Deauville has two casinos and a Louis Vuitton–flagship boutique, while Trouville is full of shabby tabacco shops and bars with bowls of recycled peanuts.) And above our table at the restaurant in Trouville hung a poster with a beautifully drawn oyster where the size had been written up in this educational way: it's the distance from the meaty oyster to the edge of the shell that's measured, not the size of the oyster. Thus, if an oyster is so gigantic that it fills the whole shell, the distance to the edge of the shell is 0. If it's teeny-tiny then the distance might be 0.5. This is all you need to remember to avoid ordering monster-molluscs, which are both scary to eat and much more expensive than the small, good varieties.

And finally, oysters are intersexual. They gender-morph themselves back and forth between "she" and "he" their whole lives. The warmer the water, the easier it is for an oyster to become a "she". And when that happens, they turn into swollen, sweaty, sunbathing preggos. The colder it is, the better the oysters. A classic rule of thumb is to only eat oysters in months that include the letter R. But you haven't really eaten oysters until you've sat beside an open window, with a beanie on, and eaten the best, freshest little cheap oysters in Paris, with your hands still damp from ice-cold saltwater and a pint of lager for 3 euro.

Annemarta Borgen finishes her chapter on oysters in *Min Fiskkokbok* with a dream of the future: that the oyster supply in the especially chilly Nordic waters will accelerate. "[Norway], the only small democracy in the world where everyone could afford to eat oysters every day!"

Ⓑ 11 arr

Chair de Poule
bar

🐾

Chair de Poule means "goosebumps". This bar lies at a nice crossroads, with a generous outdoor seating area where it's good to have a beer before continuing the walk up rue Oberkampf. The atmosphere is more taped-countertop than craft beer, but the prices are right. The music changes all the time. I've walked in to both black metal and to people standing there with a Game Boy attached to the PA system. Sometimes there's a music trivia quiz arranged by a girl who works for the radio station FIP, which is the best local station in Paris. Not because the music is so fantastic, but because the station is so loopy and eclectic that it couldn't exist anywhere else. The weirdest music I've heard on FIP was a whole piece of dialogue from the movie *Top Gun*, dubbed into Korean, followed by an hour of Wong Kar-Wai–related film music.

Chair de Poule's restrooms are up a rickety little staircase, and I always stay in the restroom for a while because the walls are covered with exciting newspaper clippings, including that very fine photo of a young Ryan McGinley when he sat naked on the ground holding a happy dachshund in his lap.

Ⓐ 141 rue Saint-Maur, 75011 Paris
Ⓣ +33 1 43 38 89 06

B 11 arr

Magazine
bar
●●●

Once you're satisfied with looking at Ryan McGinley's cherubic face in the **Chair de Poule**'s (p. 64) restroom, it's time to move on, but instead of taking the stairs back to the ground floor you can continue through the small corridor, to the unmarked door at the end. Push on the door. If it moves, that means Magazine is open. Magazine describes itself as a "dive bar", but in fact it is a super serious, English-speaking place with furnishings straight out of a French-colonial fantasy: luxurious wallpaper, and low chairs and tables. The bar manager, Mike, is a music fan: he plays everything from the band Magazine to Moondog – the blind experimental American musician who dresses like a Viking and lives on the streets of New York. The bar selection is well chosen and totally suited to a certain kind of person (me). If there are two different sorts of whiskey, one will be a cheap bourbon and the other, something from a limited edition or from a family-owned distillery that only whiskey-nerds will know.

Typical regulars at Magazine are a combination of off-duty bartenders and Irina Lăzăreanu – the Romanian-Canadian former ballerina who supported herself as a model before her other job of writing songs for rock bands began to pay off (I know, it is unfair).

Once when I was standing in line for the restroom here I started talking with a cold-wave punk-music bassist I recognized. There were only guys in the line for the women's toilet because none of them would go to the men's toilet, which is a hole in the floor. So I was given priority for the "hole". "We call them 'Turkish toilets' here", said the French bassist while pointing at the hole and snobbishly wrinkling his nose. "Interesting", I answered, "In Sweden we call them 'French toilets'". "Is that so?!" he said, shocked. "God no", I replied, "If I told people in Sweden that there's a super luxurious bar with a toilet that's a hole in the floor no one would believe me".

Just then someone came up to us and said, "The girl from Nirvana is about to play downstairs now". The girl from Nirvana? Do you mean … Dave Grohl? He dressed the right way often enough. "She with the cello.

She plays with Earth also." Is Lori Goldston one floor down? "Yes, her!" So we squeezed ourselves back downstairs, perched on one of the steps and peered between the crates while Lori Goldston dragged a chair out to the middle of the floor, took out her cello from some sort of packaging, shut her eyes and played dark vibrating music that sounded like moss growing, like the best schooled orchestra and a very naive child, simultaneously, while 50 deadly serious Frenchmen in black leather jackets stared in silence.

It can be like that in Paris sometimes.

Ⓐ **141 rue Saint-Maur, 75011 Paris**
Ⓣ **+33 1 43 38 89 06**

B 11 arr

Onze Bar

bar

After **Chair de Poule** (p. 64) you will arrive at a sort of fork: either go back a few steps to the more orderly rue Oberkampf, or turn left and continue up the hill on rue Jean-Pierre Timbaud, with its tea salons, Middle-Eastern clothing stores, faceless mannequins and rotisserie cases full of sheep skulls. I often take the left-hand route. And inevitably end up at Onze Bar.

Onze means eleven, just like the arrondissement, and it's the last outpost before you arrive in Belleville, the 20th and last arrondissement. On early, wintry afternoons, the outdoor seating at Onze is one of the cheapest places to spend many tranquil hours with the sun caressing your face. The music depends on the day: from irritating jazz to classical music I didn't know I could love. Once I heard a Romani girl play a completely original version of folk music here, seemingly unaware that she could have opened for Tim Buckley without any shame.

Just as at many of the best places in the 11th, those who work here are a mix of scabby punks, people who seem to attend any kind of labor-union meetings and Franz Kafka–types with really high hairlines.

When the outdoor temperature goes above 10 degrees Celsius, the bartender opens up the French windows facing the street so the sun finds its way to all the furniture in the dark bar.

Sometimes there's a cook here, sometimes not. But early in the evening they always serve various small snacks fished out of large tins: olives and cheese, cheese-stuffed peppers and cheese. Just like the food, the drinks are especially cheap without being bad; often there's something a little more obscure on the wine list. If it's late in the evening, or if the cook didn't turn up, you can ask if it's okay to bring takeout food instead. Because Onze is an anarchist bar, you rarely hear no for an answer. Unfortunately, most of the places nearby serve just pasty French fries and cold baguettes, and most of the patrons prioritize cigarettes over food anyway.

A 83 rue Jean-Pierre Timbaud, 75011 Paris
W onzebar.com
T +33 1 48 06 11 97

B 11 arr

Cantada II

bar

After Onze you can head back to rue Oberkampf. On the way there you'll pass the gothic-style absinthe bar Cantada II. I usually stop in and have a glass for strength before I continue further up the hill, to the really steep parties.

In the bar, absinthe bottles are stacked in several rows, and the drink is served with the classic utensils: absinthe fountain and absinthe spoon. My favorite is the small bottle with the label designed by H. R. Giger — who also designed the monster in the *Alien* movies — partly for the flavor, which is strong and good, but mostly because Giger's biomechanic creatures suit this place so well.

Later in the evening Cantada II opens its cellar; the stairs are right below the Viking doll that hangs on the far wall. The cellar is great for everyone who likes proper hard rock and doesn't feel the need to hear what the people around them are saying.

Cantada II might not be a nice, tasteful bar, but the absinthe, the Viking, the slightly outdated goth vibe, the cellar and all the forks in the road to get here make it feel like hanging around in the David Bowie film *Labyrinth*.

(A) **13 rue Moret, 75011 Paris**
(W) **cantada.net**
(T) **+33 1 48 05 96 89**

(i)
Drinking absinthe

Absinthe is a beautiful emerald green, herbal liquor with a strong flavor of anise and often a high alcohol content: that's why it's smart to dilute it with water, like pastis.

An absinthe fountain, then, is not a fountain filled with absinthe, but a fountain filled with cold water and ice. "Fountain" is maybe an exaggeration, it's more like a dispenser with a tap: one fountain per glass is usually served. But "water dispenser" just doesn't sound as cool as "absinthe fountain", and absinthe fountains are, after all, very cool.

To serve a classic glass of absinthe you also need an absinthe spoon and a sugar cube. Absinthe spoons are like a skimmer, but the size of a teaspoon. Usually the holes in the spoon are punched in an attractive way: the absinthe spoons I use at home are punched with the pattern of a skull with a bullet in the forehead. The spoons are flat, so they can balance atop a glass.

People can sometimes get really anal about the absinthe/ water ratio, but the classic way to measure is this: fill a tall, narrow glass with a few fingers of absinthe; lay the absinthe spoon over the glass's mouth and place a sugar cube on the spoon; set the absinthe fountain's spout so it calmly drips over the sugar cube. The liquor becomes opalescent and goes from emerald green to milky. When the sugar cube is almost completely melted, drop the spoon and the sugar residue into the glass, stir and drink. That's how absinthe is served at Cantada II, and often they let you have the fountain, so that you can drip in the water and decide for yourself when the drink has reached the strength you prefer.

Le Sphinx
tattoo parlour

On the way to Cantada II you'll come across an anonymous, locked door, right next to the bar **Justine**. Behind the door lies noted tattoo studio Le Sphinx, which is run by the tattooist and artist S. M. Bousille.

Once I met a sweet French girl here – girlfriend of one of the tattooists. We sat in one of the high, barred windows and joked about national stereotypes: Viking helmets and polar bears on the streets in Sweden. And I said: "Then you come to Paris, and people actually do walk around with baguettes under their arms!" She kept laughing, but I could see in her eyes that she was desperately trying to think of how she could carry home baguettes in any way other than under her arms.

Le Sphinx doesn't allow drop-ins; it's by appointment only. You arrange a time over email, then call to be let in through the locked door. If you want to be like everyone else in the 11th, go here and get a little tattoo that says "Paname", which is old slang for Paris.

Ⓐ **25 rue Moret, 75011 Paris**
Ⓦ lesphinxparis.com
Ⓣ **+33 1 58 30 35 09**

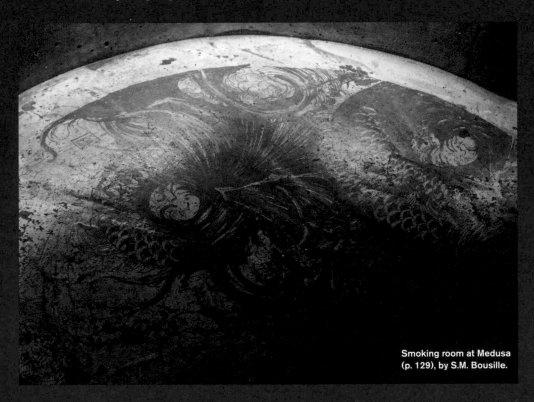

Smoking room at Medusa
(p. 129), by S.M. Bousille.

Ⓑ 20 arr

La Féline —>
La Maroquinerie
bar

"Les amateurs de rock ont le blues," ("Rock fans have got the blues"), wrote *Le Parisien* in August 2018. The reason was the wave of bar closures that swept across the 11th and 20th arrondissements. Boulevard Belleville marks the border between the two, and rue Oberkampf changes its name here to rue Ménilmontant. Precisely here lay the legendary bar La Féline. Early in the evening people would go here to dance in a serious way to garage rock, and sometimes there were live gigs. This awesome but loud music probably is the reason that La Féline is one of the many victims of the bar-deaths. Officially this was an "administrative closure", when places are forced to renovate because of non-existent fire exits and such. But at Oberkampf's surviving rock venues it's thought that the music is the real reason. Gentrification can't take rock. If you want to go to rowdy rock gigs these days you have to go even higher up the hill, to the excellent concert venue **La Maroquinerie**. But despite the fact that I love La Maroquinerie, I pine for La Féline. I've seen girls there tear off their tops and throw themselves into a fight, and sometimes a bartender would strip at the bar. I have been there both to celebrate the New Year and to mourn murdered journalists.

It's the only place I've ever had my cell phone stolen and one of the few places where I danced in public. The walls in the toilets were covered with a photo montage consisting of famous people's mugshots at a 1:1 scale, and it was always loud, crowded and judgment-free.

Ⓐ RIP La Féline, 6 rue Victor Letalle, 75020 Paris

Ⓐ Long live La Maroquinerie, 23 rue Boyer, 75020 Paris

 20 arr

Les Trois 8
beer and wine bar

La Féline (p. 71) sat precisely at the beginning of a little curve in the road where the concentration of pleasantness, even to this day, is statistically impossibly high. For those who prefer artisanal hand-crafted beverages – rather than stripteases and bar fights – the tiny little bar Les Trois 8 is a favorite. Here they serve both fancy, nerdy beers and cheap natural wines. The selection changes all the

time, and the current choices are written up on a board on the wall.

The room is ridiculously crowded, and American beer tourists share tables with bearded guys with vegetable tattoos on their arms, while messy but generous trays full of cheese and sausages from select farms appear at the bar. The baguettes are always wonderfully fluffy and the cornichons always extremely sour. It is one of those places where you actually can afford to taste several good wines, not just the cheapest, and where the fruit paste to go with the cheese is always served directly from a sticky jar labeled with freezer tape.

(A) 11 rue Victor Letalle, 75020 Paris
(W) lestrois8.fr
(T) +33 1 40 33 47 70

(B) 20 arr

Le Saint-Sauveur
bar

Sometimes I think the people who take their evil behavior really seriously must be the ones who look the least criminal; after all, it's more practical to have soft pants and nice shoes than neck tattoos and gold teeth. If this theory stands it's no coincidence that Le Saint-Sauveur lies at the end of a backstreet where no police cars ever pass.

Another advantage of this location is that people can spill out onto the street, from all the bars that lie in this little curve of the road, creating a sort of impromptu,

friendly, giant outdoor seating area with an anarchist bent.

There might, according to very unreliable information, be a documentary about the bar. It might talk about how a gang of antifascists caught on that Le Saint-Sauveur was a popular Nazi hangout and simply annexed the place. I don't know if that's true. I only know that the beer is very cheap, the atmosphere very open-minded, the playlists are varied and that the toilets are plastered with stickers from decades of different anarchist organizations. And that I love this bar a lot.

Additionally, a tip about the dress code. I know from experience that it is not a good idea to go here wearing real fur. Nobody cares that you bought it second-hand.

(A) A 11 rue des Panoyaux, 75020 Paris

Don't forget to eat!

P 11 arr

Da Vito
pizzeria

There are bars in Paris that are purely bars, where they don't serve any food at all. Also, Paris can be so distracting that you forget your basic needs, but drinking on an empty stomach can have undesirable consequences. Thus it's good to have a couple of simple food stalls for any possible bar-crawl: hamburgers, steamed dumplings, tacos, hummus. And pizza. Then again, if you have already done a bar-crawl, and forgotten to eat, this is when it's a good idea to head to the pizzeria Da Vito. If it's nice weather, take your pizza to Arsenal, the park at the nub of the canal where tourist boats go under the Bastille. But it's also fine to eat at Da Vito, too. Oh yeah, that refrigerator at the back of the place – don't be surprised if someone steps into it and disappears. There's a bar inside.

A 5 Rue Sedaine, 75011 Paris
T +33 9 50 73 12 99

R 11 arr

Café du Coin
restaurant

If you want to eat fast food with style and class, the "café on the corner" is a good alternative to **Da Vito** (p. 76). The ambition here is to be the perfect neighborhood place, and they serve drinks and snacks at reasonable prices. In the evening there's a selection of "pizzettes" – small, cheap pizzas that disappear from the table in no time. Both regulars and food tourists hang out here: people having an inexpensive three-course lunch, a quick coffee in the bar or sharing a bottle of wine. Most of the staff speak English, but say hello in French for safety's sake.

A 9 Rue Camille Desmoulins, 75011 Paris
T +33 1 48 04 82 46

R 20 arr

WenZhou
restaurant

WenZhou is a Chinese canteen, and unlike many other places in Belleville they speak fluent French here, but not many other European languages. But this doesn't matter because the menu has pictures, arrows and symbols that denote specialties (eggplant cooked in garlic), spiciness and vegetarian options. You can take food away, eat here or just buy a large hunk of fried bread for 1 euro, which you then munch on while walking along the street.

A 16 Rue de Belleville, 75020 Paris
W lacantinechinoise.fr
T +33 1 46 36 56 33

ⓡ 11 arr
East Side Burgers
burger joint

Hot dog outside East Side Burgers

The fattest burgers in town are served at East Side Burgers. There are other vegetarian burgers in Paris, at **Blend** for example, which has a really great pepper burger with masses of melted cheddar and a grilled, inverted bun. But at Blend the vegetarian burger costs 1 euro extra (because it's way more complicated to get out of the animal than beef?) and you have to listen to elevator music while you wait. At East Side Burgers the restaurant's owners stand at the cash register, and beside the counter is a photo collage with rock stars who've eaten here. Angela Gossow (lead singer of Swedish melodic death metal band Arch Enemy), a militant vegan and one of the few women in the world who growls, hangs side by side with ASAP Rocky (model, director, producer and musical alien). Sometimes a burger special will turn up on the menu, in tribute to a genre, like New York hardcore punk music. That's the only time when my tastes part ways with those of East Side Burgers.

Not too far from here there's also **Hank Vegan Burger**, but because Hank is in Le Marais, aka The Swamp (the historic section of Paris), East Side always wins. Also, everything at East Side is done by hand: the meat and bread, the cookies and quiches and the rough-cut potato fries that are cooked in the deep-fryer that sits on the counter. There is an outdoor seating area and a basement, but if both are full then you can take your hamburger to the outdoor tables at **Le 17** (p. 82), where the owners of East Side often hang out, because 17 is the perfect neighborhood bar.

On top of all that, East Side has one more major drawcard: they serve hotdogs.

There's an ongoing discussion among vegetarians regarding mock meats. Many argue that when you want to give up meat it is counterproductive to spend the rest of your life chasing after food that is "almost like meat". I have no problem with that. But I'll rarely pass up any opportunity to devour a hotdog in a bun. To me, a hotdog in a bun is a simple, warm snack that can be dressed with toppings and sauce, and eaten with one hand. There aren't any hotdog stands in Paris, with or without meat. The whole idea of food stands is unthinkable, a violation of French foodie law. And I know that enjoying the taste of a veggie-dog requires that you haven't eaten a real hotdog in a while. But when you order a veggie-dog at East Side, with several slices of melted cheddar, strong mustard and masses of fried onions (fried while you wait), this very corner is transformed into a scene from a movie, where you are just a statue standing by a shimmery red light at 8.30pm, while the leaves change color and strangers on Vespas shout to each other over traffic to get directions to the nearest bar.

A 60 boulevard Voltaire, 75011 Paris
W eastsideburgers.fr
T +33 9 67 00 78 72

R 10 arr

Best Tofu
restaurant
●

Best Tofu is on the other side of the fun but hectic crossing where boulevard Belleville changes names to boulevard de la Villette, just past Paris Store – the Asian food shop that has everything, including "exotic" goods like Worcestershire sauce and feta cheese (or "foreign sauce" and "foreign cheese", as I'm told the French call them).

Anyway.

Best Tofu is a small, oblong restaurant that serves very good fast food for no more than a song and dance, all day, every day except Thursday. The only catch is that you have to get hold of one of the low pallets that act as chairs beside one of the small fake-marble tables. And that your ass has to fit on the pallet. There are reservations (sort of), in the sense that you just go in and sit yourself down. All the pallets are movable, so nobody can get upset about sharing a table. So you sit where you sit, with your legs folded under the table, wedged between blinged-out older women and teenagers in expensive bomber jackets and Kenzo sweaters who never raise their eyes from their cell phones but still manage to order more food than I can eat in one sitting, while wealthy family men in Gucci sneakers with stuffed wheelie suitcases line up to buy a half kilo of the restaurant's own tofu (which sits in big, white plastic crates) to take away.

The first time we went here I was nervous: all the signs and menus are written with Chinese characters. So to simplify things I just ordered "something vegetarian" from our waitress. Therein followed a long conversation between the waitress and myself. I understood just three words: tofu, sweet and salty. So I ended up ordering one salty tofu for myself and one more for Stefan. That led to a hundred questions I answered with randomly selected "Yes" or "No". Which evidently was the wrong answer. For all questions. Pretty soon communication broke down so completely that our frustrated waitress finally just pointed angrily toward our neighbor's plates, the Kenzo-clad youth, and I nodded. "One or two", she asked. "One for me and one more for him across from me", I said. Which answer produced a blink that made me quickly correct myself: "Sorry, two. Just two!" It felt exactly like that scene at the beginning of *Blade Runner*, when Harrison Ford tries in vain to order four dishes from an ancient man at a noodle cart (one of my top 10 favorite food scenes in film). Then we sat there, sweating with anticipation and awaited our surprise meal. It turned out to be two bowls of enriching hot tofu soup that the waitress set down before us with a word that sounded like, "Soviant". "Ah", said we. "Soviant – now we understand. Super, that was exactly what we wanted." After one cautious bite, the tofu turned out to be so silky that it was like eating steam. On top of the tofu lay salty, chewy, black seaweed and something else that was also salty, but harder to identify. With it came two hearty bits of fried bread, which the waitress slapped down in front of us with that word, "Soviant". Doh! (*Souvient* – memory? *Souvent* – often? *Sous viande* – under the meat?) The bread pieces were the size of baguettes, but fluffy, crispy and deep-fried straight through. Since that first visit I have learned that the bread is called *yóutiáo* (pronounced you-ti-ow) in Mandarin and *yàuhjagwái* (pronounced yow-chow-kwai) in Cantonese, which doesn't help a bit. I took a detailed photo of the food and then we set upon the bowls: we gulped and burned our mouths on the salty, silky soup, eased the burn with a big bite of the golden-brown bread, and then back to the soup again, while the whole time I covertly stared through my bangs at the other guests in the place, who all seemed to know the restaurant's social code and to speak the same language as the employees.

You pay at the cash register. If you've eaten in, it's okay to go ahead of the long line of tofu-trafficking dads. When the cashier asked what we'd eaten I held out my phone. At first she looked confused, then she saw the photo, laughed in recognition and said, "That'll be five-fifty, thanks!" For two enormous portions!

The cheapest, best lunch on this side of the water, which should mean the cheapest, best lunch in the city (but I can't be sure since, I refuse to cross the river to eat lunch).

Ⓐ 9 boulevard de la Villette, 75010 Paris
Ⓣ +33 1 42 06 80 84

Ⓡ 20 arr
Dame Jane
restaurant

Here's one thing that tells me I am in a good restaurant: when one cook, with full beard and neck tattoos, explodes out of the kitchen right before dinner service with a tin of homemade paté in his hand, dips a finger in the tin and stretches it out to the other cook, who licks off the paté. And then they smile at each other like they've just shared a secret.

Dame Jane is a restaurant where the culinary ambitions are high. But it is unpretentious enough that you can dare to stick your head in and ask if they possibly have a cancellation and have a couple of seats available. Then you can finish your evening with a three-course meal, instead of finishing at **Saint-Sauveur** (p. 73).

The venue is a combination wine shop and restaurant, high on a dark street in Belleville, with a window that's already steamed up early in the evening. Someone who's good at Tetris has furnished the place, and a fixed menu is served. For those who eat anything, the evening's menu is written on the window. Those who have dietary requirements or are vegetarian should say so when booking a table in advance and then rely on the chefs.

Everything at Dame Jane feels rustic, enthusiastic and progressive, like the raw shelves of natural wine covering the walls and the food which can consist of a little of anything: boiled egg in broth, warm olives, poached cabbage wrapped in parchment – it makes no difference as long as it's good.

Don't miss the tiny restroom, either. At first I didn't grasp why there were suds in the toilet when I flushed. Then I figured it out and decided that Dame Jane's solution should become the law of the land. To save space and water, the washbasin is placed on top of the toilet tank: instead of clean drinking water, you flush with the last person's soapy water.

Ⓐ 39 rue Ramponeau, 75020 Paris
Ⓣ +33 1 80 06 45 64

Ⓡ 11 arr
Café Chilango
restaurant

Café Chilango is a small Mexican restaurant and one of the few Parisian places that uses chilli. If all the tables are full, you can eat at the narrow plank that is fastened to the wall opposite the bar. There you can stand and take big bites of cheese-covered black beans with the help of succulent Mexican flatbread. Or order a common plate to share, filled with small soft tacos topped with potatoes and bright pink sprouts, served together with a tequila shot, salt and big slices of lime.

Ⓐ 82 rue de la Folie Méricourt, 75011 Paris
Ⓣ +33 1 47 00 78 95

Ⓑ Ⓡ 11 arr
L'Orillon Bar
bar and restaurant

L'Orillon lies on the only street in this area that sometimes feels a little sketchy. At least when you try to find your way home through the alleys really late at night. These days it's rumored that the street, which shares a name with the restaurant, has become gentrified, and someone has demonstrated their disdain by scrawling "hipster bar" on L'Orillon's cracked, tiled facade.

We'd started to say, as a joke, "Where shall we go today? To the hipster bar, or … ?" Then we did, and it was super nice. And **Au Passage** (p. 10) has of course been involved in some way here, too.

L'Orillon is untouched, old-fashioned, relaxed and perfectly put together. Little flourishes on the tall glass doors remind you of Art Nouveau, and large paper bags full of freshly baked baguettes lean against the bar. Even the light is pretty and the porcelain consists of those charming, odd bowls you sometimes want to pick up at homeware stores.

L'Orillon is open all day and already at breakfast there are old men in tunics and jackets sitting and sipping coffee at the tables, while guys with computer portfolios have a *demi* at the bar. You can eat some baguette with jam, or ask if you can bring in a croissant from a bakery in the vicinity. In the afternoon you

can sit for hours at your own table and read and drink cheap wine. Or have a craft beer, delivered by a guy who himself is standing and tasting a glass while the little ones on the other side of the street rehearse their gangster moves under the pink-flowering cherry tree and cool chicks in cornrow braids who have worn themselves out on the playground come in and gulp down water in the bar before saying a polite thanks and then running out again. Snacks are served all day and all night: freshly baked bread with hummus that's so garlicky your eyes water, olives, roasted bruschetta with tomato and basil; those sort of treats. L'Orillon is your salvation when you have forgotten to eat dinner, or reserve a table, or you've spent all your money. The only downside I can come up with is that the snacks are so cheap that

I feel bad for having ordered them all and then I feel compelled to eat up every crumb.

Lunch is still unnecessary, but more luxurious. A thick layer of fish liver on a coarse bit of toast, tart mussels sprinkled over mashed potato, passionfruit coulis served in a drinking glass. The finale is a little bowl of egg and mayonnaise. I also love their radish noir – it looks like octopus ceviche, but tastes like pizza salad. If you ask nicely, you can usually get a vegetarian lunch consisting of all the sides and trimmings.

Ⓐ **35 rue de l'Orillon, 75011 Paris**
Ⓦ **lorillonbar.com**

Le 17
bar and tobacco shop
🖤

Le 17 (pronounced 'diss-sett') is the perfect neighborhood bar. It's open even on Sundays and right across the street is a laundromat, so the gang that hangs out here is mixed – mommies with their faces covered by niqabs, crust punks with scabby dogs, theater students, old alcoholics. Antoine, who sometimes works at the bar, was the first Frenchman to start saying hello to us – it's that kind of place. He also has awesome music taste and knows everything about obscure African music. Now and then Antoine abandons Paris, to move up into the mountains, but 17 is always nice. Antoine's friend and colleague Sylvain lives in a flat above the bar, and once on his birthday Sylvain made veal stew for everyone in the bar. Then we all followed him to his studio where he played and sang (in Russian) songs by Finnish rock band Leningrad Cowboys on a found piano. The bar's owner, Louise, lived her first years of life in the Swedish city Lund and on one wall hangs a child-written sign in Swedish with the prices of juice, from her very first attempt at a cafe.

It's possible to buy hot sandwiches and such at 17, but it's also totally okay to bring your own food. Now and then it happens that large families and birthday parties take over the long table at the back of the place. Some people show up with exotic, sumptuous picnic meals, while others fold up boxes of takeaway pizza.

One time we came here with a friend who plays guitar in a hard-rock band. He ordered a Long Island ice tea and Sylvain, who was behind the bar, stared in horror at him. "We don't often do Long Island ice tea. It's a very expensive drink".

The hard-rock guitarist asked, "How expensive?" Sylvain blinked his eyes and said, "One moment, I'll get my manager", and ran off to get Antoine. Then the scene was repeated. "It is a very expensive drink", said Antoine emphatically. But the hard-rock guitarist didn't give up, and the atmosphere grew tense. "Never mind that. Give me my drink! How expensive can it be?!" Antoine nervously picked at a straw, and it seemed like he was trying to figure out just how expensive an expensive drink could be, and then he said, "10 euro?" The hard-rock guitarist drank five Long Island ice teas, became friends with everyone in the outdoor seating area, besties with Sylvain, and upon closing, Antoine locked the door and began serving free beer and setting out ashtrays while everyone still there immediately began smoking indoors.

One more thing that makes 17 the perfect neighborhood bar – that makes it the neighborhood's very lungs – is that it is a tobacco shop that's open late. All times of day, wealthy women in fur pelts line up beside men with stupefying body odor to buy their beloved tobacco.

A **17 rue de la Folie Méricourt, 75011 Paris**
W **bar-le17.com**
T **+33 1 55 28 74 37**

Buying tobacco

Parisians love to smoke. I don't know why it doesn't show up in the statistics. Maybe Paris isn't representative of the rest of the country? Maybe smokers in other countries hoard more cigarettes than a living person can smoke.

In Paris people smoke with an almost rebellious disregard for life, in the most unlikely situations: on a Vespa, moving the cigarette inside the helmet with the visor set so the cigarette sticks out, which feels dangerous on so many levels; dads with babies in slings smoke at outdoor tables; and kids on school trips roll cigarettes with one hand. A very chic, young French woman in a wheelchair navigates her chair through the crazy traffic at République with one hand, the other busy holding a cigarette.

Just as Swedes go to the liquor store, Parisians make their pilgrimages to their local tobacco shop. Furthermore, many tobacco shops are closed in the evenings, and nearly all are closed on Sundays. But because Paris is a city full of loopholes, there is always one tobacco shop in each quarter that's open at night or on Sundays, and it's usually hidden on a back street. Those who live in the quarter have written in stone where the open tobacco shops are. Once you find one, the atmosphere there will be the most eclectic you've ever experienced. Like a nude beach, as the final equalizer, the tobacco shop is living proof that Parisians, regardless of income, religion or upbringing, are always first and foremost smokers.

An excursion to the 10th

Le Verre Volé la Cave

wine shop

●●●

A cave is a French wine shop. Sometimes it's also a delicatessen. Sometimes you can eat and drink in the deli. But this Le Verre Volé (there are a few versions around Paris) is no deli. Here they sell natural wines carefully chosen by a man who in the beginning we called Wine-Nazi. These days we call him Cyril, because that is his name. Cyril is so sweetly, unpretentiously polite that he makes me sick with envy of people who have actually received an education in wine. Cyril was the one who taught us that the white, almost clear La

Bohème wine is perfect with oysters, and that it is both important and fun to behave yourself. And so long as you behave yourself in his shop, he isn't dictatorial at all. The ground rule is that you must say "*Bonjour*" when you come in, and kindly also "*Bonne journée*" when you leave, if you intend to return, which you always do (there are more rules about greetings on page 88).

At Le Verre Volé la Cave there are the classic natural wines. Light, red Morgon from Marcel Lapierre, the wine growers who've devoted their entire lives to natural wine; it is my secret weapon when I offer natural wines to skeptics for the first time. Beside it is the light, red Morgon from Jean Foillard, Marcel's disciple; it works well also as an introduction to natural wines. Or Poivre et Sel, the first natural wine I drank myself, with an aftertaste of pepper. And white burgundy, more specifically Vézelay from La Cadette (more on that a little later). But there's also a whole drove of wines for next to no money at all: sipping wines, everyday wines to pair with food, table wines* and what some call in French "canon wines"**. From good to totally ok, exactly whatever wine you like. But without all the bad stuff in wine. If you feel uncertain about what you want, Cyril will give you sound, non-judgmental advice.

The name Le Verre Volé means "the stolen glass" and it's a vague reference to the '60s romantic comedy *Stolen Kisses*. The door out to rue Oberkampf is always open, except when they're closed for lunch, and the whole store smells faintly of white musk. On Friday afternoons Cyril and his friends are here sneaking tastes of wine at the cash register and hiding cigarettes under the counter while

Jacques Dutronc songs fill the space. This is as close to an imaginary happy place as a wine nerd can get.

* There are very many natural "table wines". One reason is this: in order to print the cultivation area on the wine bottle, the wine has to have certain characteristics that correspond with how wine from that region should be made and taste. Burgundy should always taste like Burgundy. And because natural wines are often so atypical, many growers don't even apply for the designation of origin because the chances are great that the answer will be "No". Instead they'll just ask a local kid to write "table wine" on a piece of paper, then the label is done and the wine's ready to drink.

** A canon is a quick glass, ideally knocked back while standing, usually of a light-drinking wine.

Ⓐ **38 rue Oberkampf, 75011 Paris**
Ⓦ **leverrevole.fr**
Ⓣ **+33 1 43 14 99 46**

Saying hello

Paris is usually described as an unfriendly city: unfriendly waiters, unfriendly people, unfriendly pigeons. But it's not so. My feeling is that Paris is one of the most polite places on Earth. And that's the problem. While you might think you've just gone into a place and ordered a coffee, you've actually insulted two or three different people in two or three different ways. So when the coffee never comes or is slammed down in front of you, it's because the other party is certain it was you who threw down the glove, and that they are only evening the score. Thus, there are a bunch of very simple tips to stick to if you want a coffee or a glass of wine without a side order of snubbing.

See that you always, always, say "*Bonjour*" when you enter a place. It is the absolute easiest, and the only, advice you really need in order to get okay service in Paris. Say "*Bonjour*" to everyone: to the shop assistant and the shoemaker, to the waitstaff and to the guys who aren't even working but just hang around in the bar at the tobacco shop all day. Not to say "*Bonjour*" is horribly rude, unforgivably unfriendly. Social outcasts, the homeless and pants-less people in foil hats who walk up to you on the street all say "*Bonjour*" before asking for money or cigarettes. So just think how low you seem if you storm into a cafe and yell "Coffee" without saying "Hi" first.

Saying "*Bonne journée*" (goodbye), when you leave is always good too.

There's also a bonus course: to adapt your "*Bonne journée*" to the time of day and year. This is basically a social sport where whoever is the most exact wins. "*Bonne journée*" applies basically until 3pm.

After that it becomes "*Bon(ne) après-midi*" (Good afternoon), for a few hours.

After sunset it becomes "*Bonne soirée*" (Good evening).

Friday to Sunday it's "*Bon weekend*". Except during major weekends and holidays, when it's "*Bonnes fêtes*" (Happy holidays); "*Bonnes Pâques*" (Happy Easter); "*Bonne fin d'année*" (Happy New Year's Eve); "*Bonne anné*" (Happy New Year); "*Bonne continuation*" (roughly so long/take care), or some other appropriate thing depending on what big weekend/holiday it is.

It doesn't end there. The classic is to wish someone who's going to eat dinner "*Bon appétit*". But if someone is going to do something difficult you wish them "*Bonne chance*" (Good luck). If it's something really challenging, you say "*Bon courage*". Swedish author Bodil Malmsten wrote about this in *The Price of Water in Finistère*. When she was out in her garden her neighbors wished her "Happy gardening", when she picked up a spade they wished her "Happy digging". When her family doctor's wife was in her ninth month of pregnancy, Bodil made her first French joke by wishing him "Happy childbirth". Or there was that one time I bought a pair of absurdly expensive egg cups at a flea market (for some reason, egg cups are in short supply in Paris). On the way out the salesperson kept repeating, "*Bo' oeu*". I didn't understand what she said at all until she clarified: she just wanted to wish me "Happy egg".

Paying

In Paris there's a very clever pricing system that nobody cares to explain. If you drink coffee at the bar it's super cheap. Inside, sitting in a proper chair at a table, it's more expensive. The most expensive is in the outdoor seating area. Thus, if you go to the bar and order a coffee in order to be helpful, and then carry it yourself to an outdoor table, you've just ripped the place off for half the price of the coffee. After that, chances are good that the staff will treat you like pond scum.

In certain places the price rises during the day so that it becomes more expensive the later it gets. The price increase is usually stated on a chalkboard inside the bar.

Prices vary greatly among different places also. As a rule, all places located on a boulevard are expensive as hell, while places that lie on back streets are cheaper. Avoid all places located at the crossroads of two boulevards.

It's a fun challenge to try to drink a coffee for just 1 euro.

I love this system because it means you can be just as poor as you like but still find a loophole that lets you have a coffee in a bar.

Getting a table

It is sometimes confusing, upon entering a restaurant or cafe, to know whether it is self-service or not. No one knows if you should order first and then sit down, save your seat with a jacket, or just plop down and hope that someone notices that you are hungry and thirsty.

In Paris all of this, of course, has been clear for a long time. The general rule at cafes, bars and simple restaurants is that you simply sit where you like. If you aren't sure if it's a simple restaurant or not, catch the eye of the waitstaff, point at a table and ask if you may sit there, then sit and wait for service. Usually this solves itself because you made eye contact and said "*Bonjour*" as soon as you came in and you noticed if someone wanted to place you at a table or not.

It is similar for outdoor seating – you just get yourself

a spot to sit (tables that are set with cutlery are reserved for dining guests). Don't worry if it takes time to get service. The basic thinking is that someone who sits at an outdoor table is there for coffee after all. I have seen Frenchmen smoke five cigarettes in 30 minutes while waiting to order coffee and then unconcernedly get up and leave.

If you're in a hurry, sit at the bar instead. This system works well with the payment system on the previous page.

R 10 arr

Le Verre Volé
wine shop and restaurant

The wine shop Verre Volé has many siblings, among them is this restaurant by the canal*, just on the other side of the border with the 10th arrondissement. The restaurant Le Verre Volé is run, confusingly enough, also by a man named Cyril (see **Le Verre Volé la Cave**, p. 86). This Cyril has wild hair and doesn't care how you behave. He becomes terror-stricken if you try to speak fake-French with him. If you speak English, he'll turn around and leave. Once Stefan tried to buy a bottle of Vézelay from Cyril. For reasons that are only known to the people who invented French, the word Vézelay is pronounced "Vay-zzehr-ley". That was not quite the way Stefan pronounced it. But Cyril said he would try to find a bottle, maybe he had one in the cellar. Then he disappeared down the stairs never to return. (The story becomes funnier if you know that Le Verre Volé's wine cellar isn't in the cellar. There's nothing down there but a water heater and a restroom with a broken doorknob). The

* In Paris "the canal" means Canal Saint-Martin, while the Seine is "the river".

90 Paris for Food Lovers

wine, a fantastic white Burgundy from the producers Domaine de la Cadette, was fished out from a shelf in the restaurant by one of the nice young waiters.

(A) **67 rue de Lancry, 75010 Paris**
(W) **leverrevole.fr**
(T) **+33 1 48 03 17 34**

Lunch is often better than dinner at Le Verre Volé, but both are fantastic. And oh yeah, never ask Cyril about a vegetarian alternative. Pretend you haven't decided yet and wait until someone else shows up. Then the cook's hands are freed and you may have some of the best vegetarian dishes in Paris. The meat dishes are rustic bordering on primitive: traditional French blood sausage with a mountain of potato gratin; a half-kilo of dandelion leaves and a half-kilo of pork chops – at least once Cyril has become sad when someone at the table couldn't manage to eat up all the fat. The fish dishes are more nuanced, often rare and with small herbs and leaves. But more bizarre things can also turn up: a bowl of mayonnaise and a bowl of whelks – the next best thing to French sea snails. Or eel and veal tartare; "Ah, a veal and eel meal deal", as our Australian friend August said when he ordered the dish for breakfast – mostly because it rhymed – which turned out to be overly ambitious.

There is no wine list at Le Verre Volé, you just explain your budget and your tastes to the waiter. All the wine can also be bought to take home. The prices on the sign apply to takeaway, so drinking on-site means a markup. And because this is a restaurant that serves perfectly chilled wine, this is where Stefan runs off to shop when I, at 8pm on a Saturday evening, decide that I want to eat 12 oysters for dinner, sitting over the kitchen sink, drinking perfectly chilled La Bohème from a Duralex glass.

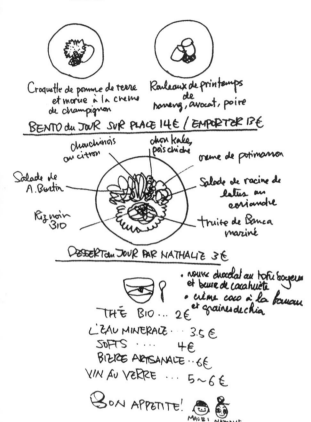

Entrée du JOUR 3€

Croquette de pomme de terre
et morue à la crème
de champignon

Rouleaux de printemps
de
hareng, avocat, poire

BENTO du JOUR SUR PLACE 14€ / EMPORTER 13€

Chouchinois
au citron

chou kale,
pois chiche

crème de potimarron

Salade de
A. Bortin

Salade de racine de
lotus au
coriandre

Riz noir
310

truite de Banca
mariné

DESSERT au JOUR PAR NATHALIE 3€

• mousse chocolat au tofu soyeux
et beurre de cacahuète
• crème coco à la banane
et graines de chia

THÉ BIO ... 2€
L'EAU MINERALE ... 3.5€
SOFTS .... 4€
BIÈRE ARTISANALE ..6€
VIN AU VERRE ... 5~6€

BON APPETITE!

MAORI NATHALIE

® 10 arr

Le Verre Volé
sur Mer

restaurant

If you took away everything that's untidy and a little wrong about the restaurant **Le Verre Volé** (p. 90), but saved the carefully prepared food, you'd have Le Verre Volé sur Mer, (The Stolen Glass on the Sea). The restaurant is

barely more than a tiled corridor – a few small tables and a raised, open bar where the food is made. Or chopped up, rather – there's a lot of raw food here.

Unlike nearly every other "natural wine and tapas" place, Verre Volé sur Mer doesn't serve tapas. They serve hors d'oeuvres. The dinner portions are very small, even for those who like small portions. But the food is so delicious that you're satisfied with just a taste. The raw ingredients have that distinct, nuanced structure but are handled with Japanese sensitivity. Fresh lettuce leaves, from bitter to peppery; wintry, pickled root vegetables, with the taste of both minerals and sugar, which a cooler climate brings out in plants; egg-cup-size portions of creamy pumpkin puree, topped with a few salted mushrooms. The fish is all caught by small boats, and dishes include some rings of nearly transparent octopus; a bowl of foamy clams; two to three slices of raw mackerel, two leaves of chervil and a teaspoon of hazy, acidic, transparent, room-temperature liquid. Once I found a wad of chickweed on my plate, forgotten under a little green salad. Chickweed is one of the world's most notorious weeds. Conventional growers panic and poison the plant as soon as they see it. I stared at the stubborn little tuft, made sure no one was looking and tossed the weed into my mouth. It was nutty, fresh and juicy. Maybe the best leaf on the whole plate. I still don't know if it was part of the dish or if I ate a bite of trash.

For lunch there's only one dish: bento, the traditional Japanese takeaway food that's served in a box. Here the bento is deconstructed, the selected dishes served on a plate. Usually a combination of salad, rice in different colors, pumpkin or root-vegetable puree, pickled onion, some interesting roasted seeds, chervil and beets in different colors, pickled and dressed in something creamy. With or without a long sliver of fish, that has been only briefly pan-seared.

For a time, many of the French reviews of Le Verre Volé sur Mer were quite brutal. But I think perhaps it didn't have much to do with the food. It was more about the letter: a completely reprehensible, but actually very funny, letter that someone in the restaurant sent to a journalist who reviewed the place when they opened. The letter was extremely French and contained phrases along the lines of, "Hope you like soup, because that's all you'll be able to eat when I'm done with you!"

Ⓐ 53 rue de Lancry, 75010 Paris
Ⓣ +33 1 48 03 21 38

Wine-Emil's Top 5

Emil Broomé has imported natural wine to Sweden since 2009, and along with Emil Arvidson he has written the book *Natural Wine*. Here are his favorite wine picks in Paris.

A quick glass
At **Saturne** you can always have a glass at the bar, if there's space. And their wine list is one of the biggest and most diverse in Paris.

Ⓐ 17 rue Notre Dame des Victoires, 75002 Paris
Ⓦ saturne-paris.fr
Ⓣ +33 1 42 60 31 90

My go-to restaurant
Out of all the times I've been to Paris, **Le Verre Volé** (p. 90) is the place I've been to most. Verre Volé got everyone to drink natural wine during the "second wave", around the year 2000. They inspired others to start doing the same thing, and here there's always something good to drink.

Always reliable
The food and wine scene is changing so much in Paris right now, but **Baratin** is old-school. They've served natural wine here for 30 years. Raquel's food is in a class of its own. Pinouche can seem like the world's sourest old man but he's begun to lighten up. After a few years of grunting he now rustles up bottles from behind the bar.

Ⓐ 3 rue Jouye-Rouve, 75020
Ⓣ +33 1 43 49 39 70

My favorite wine store
There are two. **Cave des Papilles** in the 14th was one of the very first wine shops to open. It always has such a good range of wines, from a few woven baskets on the floor with wine for 6–7 euro, but also the best, most expensive bottles. The other is **Crus et Decouvertes** on rue Paul Bert. It can be a bit regimented in Paris, with the same wines showing up everywhere, but Mikael, who owns this wine store, really takes the time to find new winemakers.

Ⓐ 35 rue Daguerre, 75014 Paris
Ⓦ lacavedespapilles.com
Ⓣ +33 1 43 20 05 74

Ⓐ 7 rue Paul Bert, 75011 Paris
Ⓣ +33 1 43 71 56 79

One wild card
Bruno Verjus has a seriously awesome wine list: awesome wines and awesome prices. You can find bottles here that aren't anywhere else. Bruno is slightly wild, an old blog-star, but also a good and humble old guy who's been around for a long time. The raw ingredients are also wild, like a fish, bought from some little village, which is only served during exactly the two weeks when it's at its very best.

Ⓐ 3 rue de Prague, 75012 Paris
Ⓦ table.paris
Ⓣ +33 1 43 43 12 26

Buying bread

One thing I love about Paris is that all the bakeries sell two types of baguette: classic and traditional (*tradi* in French). Classic is a little more modern than traditional, but not too terribly much. For a long time, all the bakeries charged 90 centime for the classic and 1 euro for the *tradi*, until they all simultaneously raised the price to 1 euro and 1,10 euro, respectively.

One year we lived in the 10th arrondissement, in a flat that was just above the world-famous, prize-winning bakery **Du Pain et Des Idées**. There they sold a third baguette, beyond classic and traditional: *comme à l'ancienne* (in the style of a damn long time ago). It was the most classic traditional of them all and also the most expensive.

Their baguette together with a small knife, a piece of Cantal cheese and a bottle of wine that the guy in the store helps open, is all you need for a perfect picnic, for instance in the **Parc des Buttes-Chaumont** (p. 142).

Eating dessert

French restaurants love dessert. Even for lunch, people are surprised if you don't order dessert: "No dessert? But it's included in the meal!" Unfortunately, the love is unrequited. Modern natural-wine places can serve fun little creations with salted caramel, sour cream, poached rhubarb and miso crumbles. But at traditional restaurants dessert is often either crunchy crème caramel or dry Paris-Brest – an incomprehensible dessert that's basically a bagel with Nutella. Or the even more incomprehensible dessert, *riz au lait* (rice pudding). It's like a French version of the Chinese starchy mush, *congee*.

Those who can do dessert, however, are the bakeries.

This dessert trick comes from Petrus Jakobsson, who runs the fantastic bakery Petrus in Stockholm. Before you go to a restaurant, go first to a bakery. Petrus is a pro, and he tends to choose one of the world-famous French pâtisseries. For me, any serious neighborhood bakery* will do. Then it's just a matter of making the tough choice between lemon meringue pie, chocolate cake with a melted-chocolate heart and tiny fruit pies with apricot, pear, apple or mirabelle (or cherry plum). Leave the pastries in your room, go to the restaurant, say no thanks to a dessert and then go home and eat all the pastries in bed, along with a bottle of natural Champagne or a cup of lavender tea, for digestion.

** What I've learned about Parisian bakeries is this: if they look good, they usually are good; also never trust a cool bakery.

B 10 arr

La Patache
bar
●

Paris gets really cold for a couple of weeks each winter. Scientists say it's a myth that you get colder in more humid climates – scientists who have obviously never been to Paris in February, when the water in the gutters has barely frozen but it's so cold that it hurts your teeth to walk around with your mouth open. There's only one thing that helps: Patache.

Patache is a bar and restaurant, but I know nothing of the restaurant. The bar sits directly across the street from **Le Verre Volé** (p. 90). In the middle of the dark brown, woodsy room stands a real wood-burning stove, and on a shelf over the stove a cute gray cat sits contentedly. Everything about Patache is warm, snuggly and welcoming. Sometimes the cat wanders over and lays itself across your knee, and often there's old scratchy soul music playing. Even the red wine, which according to French tradition should be served cool, is luke-warm at Patache. It is still tart, though. They only take cash, but their happy hour is so cheap that you can usually pay with the change you find in your pocket. Which feels sensible, because once we got here early and came upon a shamefaced bartender refilling labelled wine bottles from a BIB (bag-in-box) red wine that lay hidden under a bench against the wall.

Ⓐ 60 rue de Lancry, 75010 Paris
Ⓣ +33 1 42 08 38 92

R 10 arr

The Sunken Chip
restaurant
●

When you're out and about in the 10th arrondissement you might take the opportunity to walk along rue de Vinaigriers. The street is full of concept restaurants that might as well be called, "We will stay open for three years at the most, until the wind changes".

Trendy restaurants make me nervous. I can't stop thinking about all the renovations. How a taqueria is replaced by a hamburger joint, which is replaced by a coffee roaster, and with each new renovation the walls become thinner and thinner until the roof collapses.

But here in Paris there are also ambitiously realized concept-restaurants. Among them is the city's first, and probably only, fish and chip shop: The Sunken Chip*.

The Sunken Chip was started by chef Michael Greenwold, who used to cook at **Roseval** in Belleville – my favorite restaurant in Paris during the three seconds it was open. At Sunken Chip there's absolutely nothing vegetarian – here they serve all the fish in the world, dipped in super fluffy batter and cooked in oil. All the extras are good and well made, like thick French fries and green peas with the classic British romantic name "mushy peas".

* In Paris it's the fast-food places (rather than the hair salons) that deal in puns.

Ⓐ 39 rue des Vinaigriers, 75010 Paris
Ⓦ thesunkenchip.com
Ⓣ +33 01 53 26 74 46

C R 10 arr

Café Chez Prune

cafe and restaurant

When that terrible February cold hits, several pitstops are required if you are going to wander around the 10th arrondissement. And Chez Prune is one of the best places to warm up. Coffee in the bar, lunch, brunch, *apero** or dinner: it all works. The place is large, but still cramped and stiff in that way that only French restaurants can sustain: in one corner hangs a huge bunch of wine grapes made of what looks like papier-maché, potted plants are both lush and slumped over, and everywhere are baskets with fresh baguettes and warming plates with soup or glasses of wine. The food is home-style fare: veal, salmon and pasta, huge piles of rice, vegetables and cheese.

On winter weekends a young, bearded fishmonger opens oysters in the outdoor seating area. And during the first warm spring days, right after the terrible February cold, but before the channel that runs outside Chez Prune is littered with French students who play guitar in a way that turns me into John Belushi in *Animal House*, this is one of the best places to stop in for an early drink. When both the bar and the outdoor seating area have become chock-full, the staff turn a blind eye to people drinking in the street and balancing their Champagne glasses on the scratched-up mailbox with a view of the old arched bridge across the canal.

* *Apero* is the French word for happy hour or after-work. *Apero* stretches from whenever you leave work until you eat dinner, which can be as late as 10pm. *Apero* can include snacks, for instance a bit of cheese, but equally often it just means a drink.

A 36 rue Beaurepaire, 75010 Paris
T +33 1 42 41 30 47

ⒷⓇ 10 arr

Le Comptoir Général,

bar, restaurant and shop

🖤

On the other side of the canal from **Chez Prune** (p. 96) is Le Comptoir Général. You will find it via the little industrial area between houses, right beside a high wall covered with healthy-looking ivy and the neighborhood's second largest display of graffiti*. There is food at Le Comptoir Général, which has seemed vaguely African when I've eaten it, but I go here first and foremost to look at the potted plants that grew up through the old wooden floor, and to buy calendula oil that is cultivated and manufactured by a woman just outside Paris. I usually take time to sigh longingly over the antiques and the indigo fabrics they sell at the pricey flea market one floor up, too.

I don't want to say much more, as half the fun of Comptoir Général is the feeling of having stumbled upon a long-forgotten secret. But ... it's a good idea to go here.

* The neighborhood's largest graffiti wall is opposite *Chez Prune* (p. 96), where almost the whole side of a multistorey house is covered with painstaking, colorful scribbles.

Ⓐ **80 Quai de Jemmapes, 75010 Paris**
Ⓣ **+33 1 44 88 24 48**

Opéra National de
Paris, seven minutes
walk from Abri Soba

R 9 arr

Abri Soba
restaurant

You can sneak into this little U-shaped place for lunch or dinner. I especially like to eat lunch at the bar, where I can sit and look at the large sake bottles and tiny *kokedama* balls – those round, Japanese moss-planters that cute, ornamental seedlings grow in.

It's also possible to order small dishes before lunch – a Japanese omelet or a salad of grated radish with bonito flakes that are so thin and freshly shredded that they curl up before your eyes when they come into contact with the root vegetables. As a main course there's warm or cold soba noodles – the thick, chewy buckwheat noodles made in-house in the steamy, terraced open kitchen. They're served with salty dashi broth and various toppings, such as natto, the super fun fermented beans that stick together like a clump and are stickier than wallpaper paste.

Maybe it's the singed wooden walls and the rustic flavor of the noodles, maybe it's because the chef, Katsuaki Okiyama, looks so cool with his shaved head and baseball jersey, but I always feel like RZA in the kung fu-movie *The Man with the Iron Fists* when I eat here. Especially the scene where RZA hides out in an underground forge, surrounded by a gang of unruly youths who stand around slurping noodles, snapping up dumplings they've dropped on the floor and gnawing on steamed *baozi* buns. The whole of Abri Soba feels cinematic – to push open the huge door to the restaurant is a little like stepping into a film frame at a 1:1 scale – and other relevant references are the noodle scene at the beginning of *Blade Runner* and the dinner scene on the square in *Fellini's Roma* where an elegant woman eats snails with a hairpin.

It's also a good idea to leave a tip at Abri Soba, because you leave the tip on a fish-shaped button, on top of a beige plastic box at the checkout. The weight of the coins pushes down the fish, which causes a mechanical Japanese lucky cat to reach out and swipe the money with its paw.

A 10 rue Saulnier, 75009 Paris
T +33 1 45 23 51 68

R 10 arr

Abri
restaurant

A couple of blocks away, in a place marked by a taxi-cafe sign that says "City Café Sandwich", lies Abri – **Abri Soba**'s (p. 99) parent eatery and one of Paris' most acclaimed restaurants.

There's a hilarious review of Abri where the journalist explains that she absolutely will not question the quality of the food, but that on the other hand it is difficult to assess because it's impossible to get a table. Even if you speak French. Regardless if you email, call ahead on that same evening or stand outside Abri's doorstep ready to eat on any given day. All I can say is that it wasn't a problem to just show up and eat a four-course lunch on a weekday, or buy a sandwich on a Saturday.

Abri means something like "nook" or "cubbyhole", and the restaurant has the perfect facade: the cafe sign above the entrance is complemented by a moisture-damaged menu taped up in the window. And at the same time, when we first pushed our way through the small door, Stefan began to speak perfect French. "I want to eat here, I want to eat here", he hissed in my ear before he fluently went through several sentences in French–Japanese. Before I could take it in, we were sitting at a little table, on tiny little chairs which we scooted out gently so as not to bump into the miniature floor-altar consisting of a Buddha, quenched incense and, more puzzling, a clock.

Everything at Abri, except the food, is both shabby and elegant. Along a fast-food-like counter are sticky, Demeter-labeled bottles of French oil and vinegar in pedantic lines. Inside, Katsuaki Okiyama makes small plates that aren't shabby at all, only elegant. Around him young guys with sinewy arms toil, like slim cowboys who happened to land the wrong way around in a branding machine and ended up branded right up to their T-shirt sleeves. They call out in unison "Hai!" in answer to every inaudible instruction from Katsuaki. The restaurant itself feels like a good metaphor for the food: French stuff, Japanese touch. Like half a handful of scallops, covered with foam and peppery green leaves, which was described as horseradish by our Japanese waitress but looked like teeny-tiny wasabi leaves. Thin bites of raw fish and paper-thin pear slices stacked like a very small lasagne, sprinkled with sorrel and resting on a bed of something that tastes exactly like that creamy nut-butter you bought in packets when you were little. Black mullet with a bunch of steamed things. Steamed things never taste so good as at Abri: steamed squash, steamed black radishes and steamed scallions coated with brown mustard seeds that

crackle between your teeth and fill your mouth with a roasted, peppery flavor. All of this and a dessert, costs maybe 10 euro less than a single lunch plate at **Clown Bar** (p. 32). While we greedily scraped up every one of the crispy, sweet flakes on our dessert plates, the French headwaiter left us yet another bottle of natural Cheverny blanc from Domaine du Moulin while he chatted in Japanese with the cooks. And at the little nook where the open kitchen ends, and where yet another two dining spots were crammed in, the cook Atsushi Tanaka sat and smiled out over the controlled chaos. He looked very much like a rock star, like somebody from the Flower Travellin' Band maybe, but with a better haircut.

(A) **92 rue du Faubourg Poissonnière, 75010 Paris**
(T) **+33 1 83 97 00 00**

(B) 10 arr

Le Carillon
bar

When I feel like I'm done with the 10th, I usually take the route via Carillon back to the 11th. Carillon is located on the other side of the canal, across the vaulted bridge from the **Chez Prune** (p. 96) set. Until fairly recently Carillon was a shabby but functioning hotel, but now only the bar is left. People who go here come from the whole neighborhood: chic mothers on their way to school pickup, old Algerian men drinking coffee, people who used to sit by the canal and play guitar but who have upgraded to proper plastic chairs. The beer is as cheap as it can get and the guys in the bar wear "I ♥ Paris" shirts. In the outdoor seating the sun lingers here longest of all in the whole neighborhood and none of the employees grumbles if you move with your chair as far as you need to in order to catch the last rays. And then, when the sun has set, the four-way crossing outside the seating area fills to the brim with people and the only instructions you may have when you take your *demi* with you out into the street are: "Don't get hurt, don't break the glass". Reasonable rules of procedure and good life advice, in general. The result is the kind of place where no one jostles and everyone brings their empty glasses in again before they leave. I can't imagine that anyone has ever been kicked out of Carillon. Not even the gray cat that used to patter around the bar and safely stretched itself out on the matching gray sofa, which for some French reason looks Art Deco even though it's probably Ikea. This is a free zone, a totally unpretentious place – if bars were films, Carillon would be the French movie *The Umbrellas of Cherbourg* as made by Agnès Varda.

Ⓐ 18 rue Alibert, 75010 Paris
Ⓣ +33 1 42 39 81 88

15/11/15 2.42am

The Swedish journalist Cecilia Uddén said something on the radio about gray zones that I can't stop thinking about.

The 11th is a gray zone, but only in the physical sense. It's an elongated area between Le Marais (small, luxurious, Jewish) and huge Belleville (full of cheap Chinese food and people dressed in Middle-Eastern white robes and brand new Nikes). The 11th is the place where these two areas meet. It is the most densely populated area in Paris, in the most densely populated city in Europe. Even so, the sky is higher here, it is easier to breathe. It smells of grilled chicken and exhaust fumes, and rich and poor people from around the world give way to each other on the sidewalk. The 11th arrondissement is a good example of careful, practical co-existence. It's a little like that thing in the Middle East called hummus-consensus – essentially, "We all at least like hummus, so to heck with the rest of our differences for now".

That's how it feels in the 11th. Everyone can be who they are, as long as you don't lay into how someone else is, at least not too much. We all like hummus and drinking here. The 11th isn't Paris, the 11th is a village, a culturally self-sufficient place where someone with tape and chewing gum constantly mends and fixes cracks and problems that others say are unsolvable.

Le Carillon (p. 100), right on the border of the 11th, is a physical manifestation of all this. People drink mint tea and coffee brews at the same table. And it was here that the shootings began on Friday 13th November 2015. As an illustration of the type of place it is, there were already several nurses and doctors in the bar, because there's a hospital across the street.

Cecilia said that the reason these gray zones are attacked is because they offer an alternative to a polarized, black-and-white world. This type of place is proof that it's in fact possible to live together. Therefore the gray zone must be erased.

Right now, tonight, I am not totally sure what all of this means, but I think it means that all of these outside places, where the usual rules don't apply, are important. So very important that they are perceived as one of the worst threats in Paris, for all of those who say they love hummus, but would rather die than share it with someone else.

Staff lunch
à la Le Servan
(p. 150)

Eating breakfast

An ordinary breakfast at a place is *tartine* with *confiture*. *Tartine* is a spartan breakfast, basically a baguette cut in the "wrong" direction – so you can skip the "Will I have the bottom or top" dilemma and may just as well have both – and eaten with *confiture* (jam) or butter. A boiled egg is called "*œuf a la coque*" which for a long time I thought meant "rooster egg". At most bars and cafes that are open in the morning there's a basket of warm, buttery croissants or *pain au chocolat* on the counter also. You pick out your roll yourself and pay for it along with the coffee. The biggest challenge with a Parisian breakfast is actually the time. Once we took our Swedish friends to breakfast at our local cafe: *tartine* with *confiture* and big mugs of steaming hot *café crème*. They liked the breakfast so much that they returned the next morning and ordered the same thing. The waitress stared at them as if they had ordered her firstborn on a platter: "But, no … *C'est pas possible!*" (An impossibility!) At first they didn't understand, then they glanced at the clock and realized that it was a quarter past 10am.

Eating lunch and dinner

Food can thus be more difficult than you think in Paris. Breakfast after 10am, lunch after 2pm or dinner before 7pm is largely impossible. And if you think that it's hard to find a restaurant that's open on Sunday, then you've never tried going out to eat on a Monday. If you're bad at planning you can end up between meal times several days running. This has happened to me, and sometimes I wonder if this is the secret reason the French are all so slender.

If you absolutely must eat, look for the words "*Service continue*" outside a place, which means they serve food the whole time. And if all else fails, walk to **Le Tambour** in the touristy area around the old food market, Les Halles. Surrounded by scaffolding, street musicians and Bob Marley shirts is this little *alpite cottege* (alpine cottage) that's open practically around the clock.

One other alternative when your hunger is strong and your planning is weak is to defy your sinking blood sugar and crawl into one of the brasseries along the boulevard Belleville. There you can most often order something as unusual as crispy French fries, green salad with classic French dressing and an omelet with a light, creamy filling.

TIP

Tien Hiang

10 arr, restaurant

A good vegetarian Chinese lunch and dinner restaurant that requires you to pull in your elbows to have a seat, and abandon your decision-making anxiety – the menu is extensive, to say the least.

A 14 rue Bichat, 75010 Paris
W tien-hiang.fr
T +33 1 42 00 08 23

Ⓑ 11 arr
Black Mad Crawler
bar

As you pass this very nice bar, just at the beginning of the canal, you have brought yourself all the way back to the 11th. It's nice to celebrate by having a cheap beer at the outdoor tables, or sit at the large window and listen to rock and metal. On the walls hang odd parts from disassembled motorcycles and scooters, and along the back of the place is a half-hidden exit, perfect if for some reason you need to sneak out when someone comes in through the main entrance. It's also good to use the rear exit when you want to go around the corner to buy some unshelled peanuts from the eco-friendly food store Biocoop – Black Mad Crawler is wholly food-free and they often forget to replenish their own supply of peanuts.

Use the toilet on the left (the audience's left) if you don't want to pee with the whole line watching; the one on the right opens with the help of a fist-sized hole in the door, and the hole is placed exactly at the height of the toilet seat, which I think feels a bit too intimate.

Ⓐ 140 boulevard Richard Lenoir, 75011 Paris
Ⓣ +33 1 82 07 04 06

Ⓑ 11 arr
La Caravane
bar

Sometimes you just want to sit in a basket chair, listen to perfectly decent music and drink beer without feeling like you're being robbed. Sometimes you want to do it several times in a row. Sometimes you want shrimp chips with it. Sometimes you'll let a coffee suffice for four hours because your internet

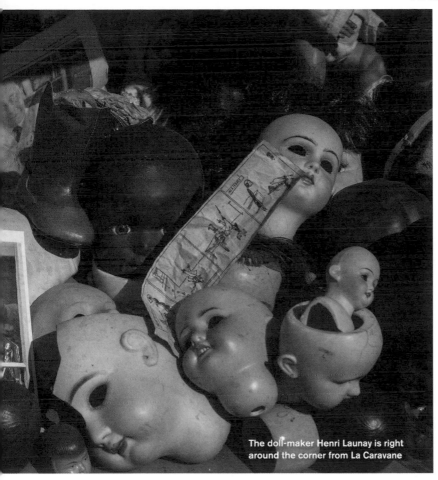

The doll-maker Henri Launay is right around the corner from La Caravane

died right in the middle of a panic-deadline and all you want is a little free wifi and no fuss. All of these things you can do at Caravane. It's possible to eat here too. The food is some form of DIY-fusion, and it is often full at lunch and dinner. There is absolutely nothing wrong with the kitchen, but that isn't the reason I continue to come here. I go to Caravane because everything is as it should be. Caravane is not perfect. It is the opposite of imperfect: a place so free of shortcomings and sources of irritation that all moods and all days are potentially Caravane days.

Also don't miss the chance to peek at Caravane's funny little delivery truck, which stands outside the window. It grows more and more graffiti-covered with every passing year since I first saw it, sometime in the early 2000s.

A 35 rue de la Fontaine au Roi, 75011 Paris
W lacaravane.eu
T +33 1 49 23 01 86

A trip south
/ rue de Charonne

Septime la Cave

wine bar and wine shop

If Oberkampf and Jean-Pierre Timbaud are your best drinking buddies, then rue de Charonne is who you want to have dinner with. This is the street that Pater Terrier runs along when he desperately tries to get rid of the foundling Grenouille in the book *Perfume*. It describes the area then, in 1749, as "far, far outside of town". Now it's right in the middle of things if you're craving natural wine and tapas.

Across the street from Septime la Cave is the swish restaurant **Septime** which I think is old-fashioned and overrated: too many personnel and too much brown in the food. Septime La Cave is the restaurant's more relaxed "back pocket", and of course a *cave* is, as we already know, a wine shop. But this wine shop happens to be of the type where you can both taste wine and eat a bit of food. There are different kinds of alcohol licenses in France, and Septime la Cave has one that resembles Old Sweden's beer-sandwich license: where every place that serves beer had a sandwich that everyone who wanted to drink beer was forced to order – no one touched this sandwich, it just went back and forth between the kitchen and the beer-buyer. The difference is of course that at Septime la Cave there's never a crumb left of the little snacks they serve. Last time I was here there was a new sommelier in the bar and he said nothing about food so I asked if the dining requirement had been abolished. Or, literally, "One doesn't need to eat?", because that is as far as my French goes. The sommelier answered, with the tourist-friendly service staff's catatonic pained expression: "That you may determine for yourself, madame". He thought I was asking him if I was hungry. Anyway I suppose that Septime la Cave must have a proper alcohol license now. There is still food, though. Both enormously simple and pretty sick things come out from beneath the counter: small bits of duck liver wrapped in eel, tiny fish in oil or the best cornichons I've eaten. All of it is served together with a never-ending plate stacked full of thin slices of tart toasted bread. You can eat the snacks in the little bar, or sitting at an upside-down wooden crate with your back against one of the tall cabinets full of natural wine.

One bad thing about Septime la Cave is it's quite popular with wine tourists, including tour guides with loud voices. In that case, just leave. Or possibly take a glass with you to the little plank mounted outside the window, recessed into the wooden facade that looks like something left over from a forest fire caused by a minor volcanic eruption. From there it's possible to watch the strange anarchists inside **Holy Holster** (p. 110) from a safe distance, or enjoy the sight of the mighty, adult ivy that spills out from a courtyard and is on its way to devouring a whole wall further down the street. An unscientific investigation (by my own pocketbook) says that it's better to drink wine by the glass than to buy a bottle from here: the mark-up seems larger than at, for instance, **Verre Volé** (p. 86).

Ⓐ 3 rue Basfroi, 75011 Paris
Ⓦ septime-charonne.fr
Ⓣ +33 1 43 67 14 87

ⓦⓢ Ⓑ 11 arr

L'Incognito
wine shop and bar

When you've drunk and snacked enough at **Septime la Cave** (p. 108) you can continue directly across the street, to the secret little bar L'Incognito. L'Incognito used to be extremely incognito – hidden behind a black, unmarked door. The new door has a glass window and is easier to find. But before you go in there, go into the wine shop right around the corner, on rue de Charonne. Here are excellent natural wines by the glass, craft-brewed beer in bottles and cheeses that go from mildly salty to penicillin-strength moldy. You order what you want, leave the shop empty-handed, saunter back around the corner and in through the little secret door. The guy in the shop arrives through a back door, with your order. Last time I was at L'Incognito there was a stereo that you could plug your telephone into, so you could play your own music. And when the smokers on the street got too loud for the neighbors the ashtrays were taken from the tables and the whole party moved indoors instead. The restroom lacked even a sink, so

I always used to hesitate before peeing – or shaking hands with someone – here. Recently L'Incognito renovated considerably, and I slightly miss the play between dive and swish.

Because L'Incognito is also a shop, it is just as good to buy bottles to take home. Those who dare to go up the rickety spiral stairs behind the cheese counter will find a very nerdy assortment of beer from around the world, at very reasonable prices. Stefan is especially fond of sour beers, among others the ones called lambic, which we were persuaded to buy the first time we were here at L'Incognito. They're unfiltered and brewed with wild yeast flavored with so much citrus that you can be fooled into thinking you're drinking lemonade on a warm summer evening.

A **71 rue de Charonne, 75011 Paris**
(the door to the bar is on rue de Basfroi)
T **+33 1 43 72 06 34**

B 11 arr
Holy Holster
dive bar

Alright, this is absolutely not an elite bar, but it can be difficult to hear harder rock and punk in Paris, and this is one of the more reliable places. Don't let it deter you that half the bathroom door is missing*. Or that the bartender looks like Alex in *A Clockwork Orange* and knows it. He hangs with a company of young anarchists who're still dressed by their mothers and old punks with drooping mohawks who stare with open hostility, unblinking and unashamed. Now and then someone with a dog on a rope tied around his waist sticks his head in and says "Hi". On one wall hangs the bar's T-shirts: a surprisingly wide range for a place that next to no one goes to and where those who sit at the bar don't actually seem to have enough for a super cheap beer. I long for a Holy Holster T-shirt with a picture of a sexy oyster with a pearl in its mouth and the words (oh, how I hope that I don't find this!): Shuck and swallow.

I can't imagine that it would work to speak English at Holy Holster, but I have never felt quite energetic enough to test that. If it's too loud and crowded at L'Incognito you can be guaranteed to find ... maybe not peace and quiet here, but solitude, at least.

* For being a culture where everyone goes out to drink wine, coffee and various other diuretic things, doors are surprisingly under-represented in the context of restrooms. Maybe everyone has been drinking diuretics for so long that they are now completely dehydrated? That would explain why there's never a line for the women's room in Paris.

A **4 rue Basfroi, 75011 Paris**
T **+33 1 40 24 18 80**

R 11 arr
Clamato
restaurant

When you've finished with **Septime La Cave** (p. 108), **L'Incognito** (p. 109) and **Holy Holster** (p. 110) you can continue across the street to a real dinner at Clamato, which also belongs to **Septime**. It is a modern and extremely English-speaking fish and seafood restaurant with many vegetarian dishes.

For budget-friendly options,
see Baron Rouge (p. 127)

Paris — squeeze in at the still-packed bar, and order a whole bucket of oysters and a bottle of minerally, almost salty, natural white wine.

The only thing that can disturb me here, and at other popular natural-wine-and-tapas places, is that the waiters sometimes try to bully you into ordering more food than you want, because they assume that you've never been to a natural-wine-and-tapas place before. Also that they get angry when you refuse to share your plate with the rest of the table. It feels like going to middle school in a hippie collective, but with a bill for many hundred euros.

(A) 80 rue de Charonne, 75011 Paris
(W) septime-charonne.fr
(T) +33 1 43 72 74 53

Here I once heard an American tourist say to one of the girls on staff, "Your English is very good", and gave her a thumbs-up. She responded: "Mhm, I'm from Chicago".

Clamato is extra cool because it doesn't take reservations. But because you are on time (or rather, the French are generally late), you get here an hour earlier than the French, who show up at 8pm. Thus you can usually get a table, even if you decide at the last second that you want to go out to eat dinner.

It's possible to eat a dinner consisting of several small plates, which are often prepared and arranged in a way that makes it easy for everyone around the table to have a little. Another alternative is to show up late — which essentially means close to midnight in

(S) 11 arr

Maison POS
food shop
🐾🐾🐾

Just like anywhere, the organic food shops in Paris often feel like upper-class communes. But there are alternatives. Like Maison POS, an austere little eco-store, no bigger than a carport, with things that are grown and made by small, sustainable farms as close to Paris as possible. And because Maison POS functions as a wholesaler, without the middleman, prices are so low that anyone can shop here. The store is missing both a door and a heater, and it opens at unpredictable times each day. But it sells the very best butter — cheaper than at the supermarket and wrapped up in baking paper — and also the cheapest, loveliest small oysters – a dozen for 9 euro. And goat yoghurt; don't forget the goat yoghurt! Like eating a mild chèvre with a spoon. It's made by Chèvrerie St Cosme, which in my mind translates to St Cosmo's Goat Farm, and there's a hot pink, psychedelic goat on the jar.

If you've managed to skip lunch, it's good to swing in to Maison POS and buy a fat paper packet of empanadas (small Portuguese dumplings made of crisp dough, filled with feta cheese and spinach), a handful of dried dates and a bottle of unfiltered cider with a label drawn by the apple-growers' children. If you walk to the left out of the store and then take the first street to the left, down to rue Charrière, you'll come to the square Raoul Nordling, named after a French-Swedish war hero who protected and freed thousands of

prisoners during WWII. There are a couple of cute mini parks here that are so secluded you can nearly always find a free park bench to eat your picnic on.

A 90 rue de Charonne, 75011 Paris
T +33 9 81 72 37 80

TIPS

Chez Paul
11 arr, bar

This is probably the most traditional French place in the whole book. Here there's a telephone kiosk, a loud matron and a single vegetarian dish: a plate filled with the sides that go with meat and fish dishes. Other dishes are perfect for a hard-working fisherman from the 1800s.

A 13 rue de Charonne, 75011 Paris
W chezpaul.com
T +33 1 47 00 34 57

Buffet
11 arr, restaurant

This is *not* a buffet. It's just that one owner happens to be Jean Charles Buffet, from **Au Passage** (p. 10). He and Audrey started Buffet as a tribute to their grandmother's cooking. Here they serve traditional French dishes like *oeufs* mayonnaise (the classic egg mayonnaise), beluga lentils with cabbage and, um, fish and chips. The customers are familiar and the tables are so close together that you have to suck in both your stomach and your rear. Everyone *wants* to speak English, and even if they don't always succeed, you can always make yourself understood.

A 8 Rue de la Main d'Or, 75011 Paris
W restaurantbuffet.fr
T +33 1 83 89 63 82

11 arr

The Bottle Shop
bar and restaurant

🐾🐾🐾

The bars Bottle Shop, **Stolly's** (p. 135) and **Lizard Lounge** (in the 3rd arrondissement) are owned by an Anglophone. This means all the staff speak English. It also means that the usual French rules of table service are replaced by the English order-at-the-bar rule.

On Sundays I go to Bottle Shop to eat brunch and try to spy on Jane Birkin's daughter Lou Doillon. The brunch plates overflow with poached eggs and bagels, burritos and black beans, and the drinks are dangerously strong. The coffee is served *sans fond* (in a bottomless cup); it's what we Swedes would call Swedish coffee: unlimited refills of brewed coffee. But you have to arrive early because from 2 or 3pm it becomes child-chaos. That is really only ever a problem on Sundays, the only day of the week that a French child affects another restaurant customer's experience, because Sundays belong to families and children in Paris. It's just good to know that it happens, so you can prepare yourself.

All the other days we go to Bottle Shop to use the internet, listen to music, read the news in silence, drink cheap beer during happy hour or eat heaping bowls of creamy pasta for lunch. Late at night it can be very hectic here, and the bar manager Antoine handles Parisians' love of cocktails like a soldier in the trenches. I have never seen anyone work so hard.

Antoine was also one of the very first Frenchmen who spoke with us: he came over

to our table, slapped down his enormous, tattooed hand between our open newspapers and shouted, "You two! You are the quietest Swedes I've met in my whole life!" Then he stormed back to the bar and continued shaking drinks at 250 BPM. We have been friends ever since. We also often go to Bottle Shop to chat with Rose, the strawberry-blonde Polish bartender with Buddhist inclinations and an endless amount of hair-raising stories. It is a perfect place to have an early aperitif, a cup of tea or a *Ti' punch* in the outdoor seating area, for example. That last is pronounced 'tee-ponch' approximately, with emphasis on the last syllable, and is a short cocktail of lime wedges, cane sugar and rum, served in a Duralex glass. It doesn't matter if it's some slightly low-grade rum, cheap and light.

If you manage to hang in there at Bottle Shop until closing, which is unlikely, because Antoine starts serving Jäger bombs a bit into the evening, you can put your leftover drink in a plastic to-go mug before you're sent home.

In winter it's important not to lay your jacket on top of the heating element. They are large, pretty and ancient, and the heat is waterborne, but I suspect the water is 100 degrees and all who come into contact with it will melt or be scalded.

(A) 5 rue Trousseau, 75011 Paris
(W) cheapblonde.com
(T) +33 1 43 14 28 04

Ⓑ 11 arr

Red House
bar
🐾🐾🐾

When people who work at **Bottle Shop** (p. 117) aren't working at Bottle Shop they go to Red House to play pinball and sip on meticulously blended drinks. The bar is in an anonymous but bright red building, on a small back street that you'll miss if you blink. Inside the door the room is crammed with buffalo heads, candles with Catholic saints' pictures, knickknacks and the world's most obscure liquor bottles. There is always good music, and often different themes. Even though Red House doesn't serve food as a rule, the night's theme can be anything from tacos and karaoke to chicken wings and an important American sports match. The staff also speak English – Joe from Texas and Jen from Manchester create a beautiful symphony of dialects behind the bar.

One totally ordinary evening when we slipped into Red House to have a quick beer on the way home, James Henry, from the fine restaurant **Jones** (p. 18), was there making smørrebrød in the bar. While he prepared the sandwiches he told us that he had just been on a road trip – from Lappland to Galicia (Spain), which took just a few days. The bread was dark and covered with different combinations of seaweed, roe, smoked fish, fresh cheese, chives and dill. "Take a sandwich first", said James, "then pickles", (a pickled yellow beet or a cornichon depending on the toppings), "finish with a *snaps*", (a shot of vodka). The vodka in the glass was cloudy and almost syrupy; one *snaps* tasted strong and sweetly of cucumber, the other of fennel seeds. I sipped at the *snaps* and took a gulp out of my beer bottle to wash down the heat. After that, the intense sweetness moved to the bottle, like some sort of unwitting example of that modern metaphysical cooking that involves smoke, steam and other volatile ingredients. The bottle continued to taste faintly of licorice perfume the rest of the evening, which ended with me standing in a corner and shouting in the ear of a rockstar while a small Mexican hard-rocker tried in vain to reach the bar on the other side of the crowd and a nervous guy with serious dreadlocks seemed to propose to his shocked girl. She stared dizzily at the 50 white roses he held out while their friends stood and crossed their fingers, hidden in the back corner. It went well, I think.

Both Red House and Bottle Shop make me think of Frenchwomen's hair. In no other place in the world can you see such carefully tousled hair ("What do you mean? It was like this when I woke up, I swear!"). That's how the best bars feel, too. What looks casual, charming and a little worn is in fact the result of hard work. It's a bit like a good song: the simplest is the most difficult, and nothing is so hard as to make something difficult look easy. Red House feels like that. The only thing that makes you feel the effort are the prices, which means I have to take small, well balanced breaks between visits here.

One last thing: Red House serves a gourmet version of a Pickleback. The drink consists of a shot of whisky and a shot of pickling liquid, which you drink in the same way as moonshine and soda in a car in Norrland — one at a time, right to left. All the French bartenders I spoke with, regardless of origin, claim that Pickleback is incredibly beneficial. It's something to do with the body's acid-base balance and the electrolytes in the pickling liquid. Red House makes its own pickles — crispy gherkins, hot chilies, small peppers — and each time a jar of pickles is finished they toss the leftover liquid into a common collection bottle. It is the contents of this blended bottle that then becomes the other half of their very potent Pickleback.

Ⓐ bis 1 rue de la Forge Royale, 75011 Paris
Ⓣ +33 1 43 67 06 43

Speaking French

People often ask me how much French I really speak. And instead of saying "a little bit", I thought I'd illustrate with some examples.

Among other things I have:

- Said to old ladies who held open doors for me, and men who picked up dropped mittens for me, that they were very handsome, instead of very kind.

- Asked a bartender if I could please buy some nets from him, instead of some nuts. Afterwards I found out that peanuts aren't called nuts in French but *cacahuète*, which is my favorite French food word after *topinambour* (Jerusalem artichoke) and *barbe à papa* (cotton candy or literally "Pappa's beard").

- Asked a bartender to listen to my bag while I went to the toilet, rather than look after my bag while I went to the toilet.

- Ordered toe soup, instead of nettle soup.

All the French took this very well (with the exception of the guy I ordered toe soup from, who stopped, stared horror-stricken at me and said, "*WHAT* did you say you want?!").

Not speaking French

Achilles is a Finnish designer, son of a stonemason, and for many years has lived in his own house at the beautiful Parc des Buttes-Chaumont. He says that the very most Parisian you can be, obviously, is to refuse to learn to speak French. He speaks English instead with a strong French accent and never has any problem making himself understood.

© ® 11 arr

Mokonuts Café and Bakery

cafe and restaurant

Do you know what halvah is? I began to wonder, one morning in March after I got a press release from an underwear brand, if everyone should eat more halvah. I remember it clearly, because it was the same day that I missed two deadlines, posed a simple but urgent question to the Central Statistics Bureau and got an answer of ten pages that among other things included the sentence "Sending with some chapters from the book *Agriculture in Numbers*, years 1866–2007". After that I dropped a goat-yogurt on the floor and discovered a weird birthmark. By then somehow it was already afternoon, and the only reasonable thing was to chuck it all and eat cake. When I got to the cafe-bakery Mokonuts I pointed at a sweet loaf that lay on the counter, that looked unusually nice, and asked what was the flavor of the *gâteau du jour* (the cake of the day). "That, that is halvah", answered Moko knowingly, "That is every day's cake". And because you should always do as serendipity tells you to, halvah it was. And because serendipity is always right it turned out that halvah is one of the best cakes ever. The name comes from the Arabic word

halwah which means "sweet", and Mokonuts' own version is both sweet and succulent, even creamy, and chock-full of walnuts and crispy bits.

To look in through the window at Mokonuts can sometimes be a little off-putting. It is a fine cafe furnished in light-coloured wood and thus draws a large clientele that we can call "youths with laptops". But it is worth braving the youths and staking out a corner. The reward comes in the form of various inventive baked goods, treated with an elite kitchen's seriousness but served with cafe Moko's humor: feta cookies flavored with chai spices; crumbly cookies with salt-toasted muesli and bitter chocolate; soft cakes filled with crispy seeds, lemon and grapefruit and then brushed with a sticky liquor just before serving, which

MOKO'S OLIVE OIL AND YOGHURT CAKE

Cake batter
4 oz (120 g) olive oil
3 eggs
4½ oz (125 g) yogurt
2 oz (60 g) lemon or orange juice
3½ oz (100 g) sour cream
5 oz (140 g) superfine (caster) sugar
7 oz (200 g) flour (any type,
  i.e. spelt, etc.)
1 teaspoon baking powder
2 tablespoons poppyseeds or
  other seeds
10½ oz (300 g) chopped seasonal fruit
  (citrus, cherries, nectarines, etc.)
zest of 1 lemon

Topping
3 oz (95 g) rye or whole-wheat flour
2 oz (60 g) superfine (caster) sugar
3 tablespoons (45 g) oats
4 teaspoons (20 g) poppyseeds or
  other seeds
2 fl oz (55 g) olive oil

Preheat the oven to 350 degrees F (180 degrees C). Butter and flour a loaf pan (tin). Make the topping by combining all the ingredients in a bowl and, using your hands, blend them into a crumbly paste. Set aside.

In another bowl mix together the olive oil, eggs, yogurt, juice and sour cream. Combine the dry ingredients in a separate bowl, then add them to the egg mixture. Stir in half the chopped fruit and the lemon zest, and pour the mixture into the loaf pan (tin). Spread the rest of the fruit over the top — this prevents all the fruit from sinking to the bottom. Crumble the topping mixture over the fruit and bake on the middle oven rack for about an hour.

makes them criminally moist. Moko's husband, the cook Omar, stands in the little open kitchen and cooks food from produce grown at two small farms just outside Paris. Sometimes their small child sits on the cake counter and does that cool thing some kids do: respond unhesitatingly in every language spoken to her. On the high, narrow shelves are natural wines in red, white and orange, and in a bowl are pretty, uneven garlic bulbs where each stalk was clipped by hand.

Moko and Omar are also two cooks who name-check their *maraîcher*, their market suppliers*, when they talk about their food. Moko and Omar both come from prestigious restaurants but now, when they opened their own, they choose to scale down and be present, just like many other cooks in Paris. It makes me happy and warm inside, and not so squeamish.

I usually skip coffee at Mokonuts and have a tart, pink infusion of grapefruit and rosemary instead. It is served scalding hot in a thin glass mug so that the pink flavor seeps in through as many senses as possible. And it so happens that the infusion goes perfectly with halvah.

One additional fun detail: now and then people come in and ask about donuts, to Moko's great surprise. The name of the cafe has nothing to do with donuts, but is Moko's nickname from when she was little. I cross my fingers that she will expand the business and that her next place will be called Loco Moko.

* They are Thierry and Elise Riant and Marie Brouard.

A 5 rue Saint-Bernard, 75011 Paris
T +33 09 80 81 82 85

Le Jardin Nomade
community garden

As soon as you try to get somewhere in the area around **The Bottle Shop** (p. 117), **Red House** (p. 119) and **Mokonuts** (p. 122) you will inevitably find yourself standing wide-eyed in front of Le Jardin Nomade – the little enclosed community garden surrounded by graffitied walls. There are around 200 community gardens in Paris, and more are added all the time because the city has created a system where everyone who discovers a bit of unused or abandoned land can apply to build a *jardin partagé*, a shared community garden.

It hasn't always been this way. The tradition is new, and it all began with Le Jardin Nomade and the elderly couple Ève and Bernard. They live in the neighborhood and were tired of developers who bought demolition sites and either did nothing with the building or sold the lot. The area would deteriorate, eventually dragging the whole neighborhood with it. So Ève and Bernard set up a kind of approved occupation. This is why the gardens are called *Nomade*. The property is still in theory occupied, and the garden can at any time be commandeered back from the growers if the developer should settle its tax debt (or whatever it was that made them disappear without a trace), show up again and decide to build their building.

Until then, Ève continues to cultivate her 1 × 1 square meter lot, full of salvia she uses for spicing her Normandy-style wine, and flowers from A to Z, while local kids can learn how to grow vegetables in anything from a broken wheelbarrow to an old plastic bottle.

The garden is open to the public a couple of days a week. Some evenings during autumn and spring the growers throw a party for everyone in the neighborhood. Then lights and lanterns light up the tiny little garden, warm wine and chocolate are offered, and the growers sing French songs from the revolution. Look for the dates on noticeboards, or the website.

Ⓐ **48 rue Trousseau, 75011 Paris**
Ⓦ **qsb11.org**

WB R 12 arr

Le Baron Rouge
wine bar and restaurant

A couple of blocks away from rue de Charonne is Baron Rouge. On Sundays it is obligatory to eat oysters for breakfast outside the little bar – it is only open between 10am and 4pm, so you have to be quick. The wine is cheap and served *en vrac**, on tap, which usually gives the French the vapors. Buy a glass, a carafe or a bottle of white at the bar. Muscadet for example. Take the bottle and a glass out onto the street. There, a fishmonger stands and swings an iron bar that is loosely screwed onto a chopping block at one end and has a spike attached at the other end. With the spike he opens oyster after oyster, while people gather, set their wine bottles on trashcans and car hoods, and slurp up the mollusks. The products are not perfect, but Baron Rouge creates that thrilling feeling that you can do more or less whatever you want. Already by early afternoon the whole street is full of little old ladies who slowly chew oysters as big as they are, American tourists who are cross-eyed with exaltation and one or two local ice queens in moth-eaten, endangered furs.

The restroom is located in an unheated shed in the courtyard and consists of the classic hole in the floor with two footprints on either side. You can wash your hands with the garden hose in the yard.

* Usually things like grain, sugar and nuts are sold *en vrac* (in bulk) in France. When you shop in bulk you can return your old sugar packet time after time, and because it is wholesale the prices are well below that of packaged goods.

A 1 rue Théophile Roussel, 75012 Paris
W lebaronrouge.net
T +33 1 43 43 14 32

Some Girls

bar

If you are done exploring the area around rue de Charonne, it's time to move on toward rue de la Roquette. The closest route is, believe it or not, via rue de Lappe. That's where you'll find Some Girls. It's a fun, totally ordinary bar where they play a lot of Rolling Stones, but the difference between this and all the other bars in Paris is that they play more than just "Paint it Black" and "She's a Rainbow".

The biggest reason to stop by here is actually not the bar, but the street: rue de Lappe. It can be pretty seedy and sketchy here, but on this street there used to be a bar where the well-known psychomagician and filmmaker Alejandro Jodorowsky gave free tarot-card readings. Here too, oddly enough, is the fine-dining restaurant **Chez Paul** (p. 115).

Ⓐ 43 rue de Lappe, 75011 Paris
Ⓣ +33 1 48 06 40 33

Café de l'Industrie

cafe, bar and restaurant

This corner is fairly teeming with places called Café de l'Industrie. The nicest of them is the biggest, Café de l'Industrie at number 16.

The main selling point with this Café de l'Industrie is that you can always, always find a seat and you always, always get what you expect, which, so long as you don't have excessively high expectations, is not half bad. A glass of pastis or a coffee or both. Maybe a plate of French fries. As long as you are surrounded by dusty palm plants, books, antique birdcages, salon-style paintings, ancient ceiling lamps and tall French doors, you don't need much more.

Ⓐ 16 rue Saint-Sabin, 75011 Paris
Ⓦ cafedelindustrieparis.fr
Ⓣ +33 1 47 00 13 53

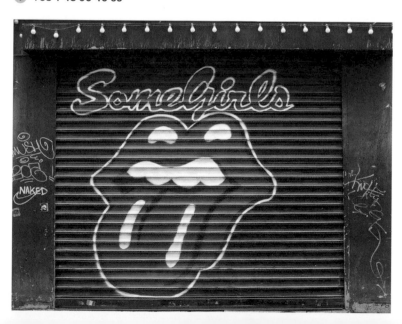

Ⓑ 11 arr

Medusa
bar

Medusa is a little rock bar run by a gang of young, disheveled guys who all eventually turn out to have a little ("little") house ("house") in Normandy. They all love light beer and speak perfect English. The tattoo artist from **Le Sphinx** (p. 70), Sébastien Mathieu, has painted the Kraken-inspired figures that cover the walls, floor and the sink inside the privy. The music is well-chosen rock, from Electric Wizard–doom to Bob Wayne–country. There is a cheese plate with thickly sliced, salty pieces of cheddar, toasted sourdough bread and sweet-and-sour red-onion chutney. The cheese plate goes well with several small glasses of natural wine.

Medusa is as far as you can get from a pretentious cocktail bar, but nevertheless happens to be a very good cocktail bar. Guy, who owns the bar, believes that you don't have to do business just because you're good at what you do: that *everything* you do in life should be done with love and integrity, not pride; then everything is always well-made, nature-friendly and fair. This is the reason that guests with a tight budget can buy a cheap bottle of Moosehead beer and a Gammel Dansk (a Danish liquor), while the connoisseurs can order some incomprehensibly complicated drink that includes absinthe, bourbon and bitters made by hand in the bar.

Far into the space is a beautiful smoking room, lit solely by candles, so that the neighbors would not be disturbed by the smokers. Late at night the little bar fills up wall to wall, but around 6 or 7pm there's still plenty of room.

Here I have seen Guy and his friend Pierre make their own hibiscus infusion on a little warming plate in the bar. They spiced a reddish-black, sour juice with essence of orange flower while they explained the recipe for the historic French drink *Cimetière* (Cemetery). Here's how to do it. You know how most bars have a plastic mat with deep grooves, or a shallow, oblong metal tub sunk into the bar? That's where you set all the beer glasses, drinks and shots that are on their way out to the bar, so spills are captured and don't spread out across the entire bar. At the end of the night you carefully pick up the tub and tip the contents into a large beer glass. That is a *Cimetière*.

To me this type of 360-degree knowledge is proof that someone is a really good bartender.

We were also in here one time, on the second day of an endless state of emergency, with locked doors and darkened blackout curtains, the interior lit by tea lights, while panic-stricken people ran along the street outside and Guy and the others fetched people in through the exit to the garbage room, so that they could huddle up in safety together with us in the darkened space. Afterward I learned that it was a false alarm, it was only someone who decided to set off a firework at the place de la République during the memorial of the November 13 attacks. We went home on unsteady legs through the empty streets, glad that we in any case had spent the evening among people who would quickly become our friends.

I love Medusa a lot.

Ⓐ 48 rue Basfroi, 75011 Paris
Ⓦ medusaparis.com

SMOKEY MANHATTAN

I asked Guy for the recipe for "that drink I like, that tastes a little of boat tar", and this was what he wrote down.

5 cl Laphroaig 10 year old whisky
2 cl Martelletti Vermouth Classico
2 dashes Angostura Bitters

Stir the ingredients in a shaker with ice and pour into a cocktail or martini glass. Squeeze a bit of orange peel over it, and toss the peel.

This is a twist on a Manhattan. It is smokey thanks to the whisky. It is a classic cocktail, and not especially original, but you'll like it! Less is more!

ⓒ 11 arr

Chez Aline
cafe

This is a tiny little, rundown fast-food place, barely more than a kiosk, which is easy to miss where it lies tucked-in between a halal-butcher, parking lot and pinball bar. Look for the neon-lit horse that sticks out from the facade, which shows that Chez Aline used to be a horse-butcher. Here they serve a much better lunch than what you would guess when you walk past, but at prices just as low as you'd expect. They have fine natural wines and a well-chosen selection of beers and sodas.

The food is simple and unadorned. The menu is handwritten. You find it on the bare stone wall outside the kiosk, because it's the only place where there's enough space to read – which I never succeed with because the menu is written in that style of handwriting that seems to be taught with Chinese gymnastics-level discipline to all French schoolchildren. Here is an abbreviated transcription. Begin with choosing between two different types of bread, either a *tradi* baguette or "round bread with sesame seeds on top", known in the rest of the world as a "hamburger bun". The bread is freshly baked, the baguettes are a little coarser and chewier while the hamburger bun is like a more substantial brioche. When the bread is chosen, you fill it with … filling. It doesn't make much difference what it is, you can just say *végétarienne* (vegetarian) or point at the optional flavor combinations on the extra menu inside the door. Whatever the choice, you'll get a sandwich packed full of different pickled goodies, colorful shredded carrots, cheese and perfectly dressed lettuce leaves. And also a bit of fat, juicy frittata. All wrapped up in paper and put in a packet to takeaway.

You can eat here also, although it's better if there's not more than two of you. It is, as mentioned, very tight for space. Once when I ate lunch here I saw a cook try in vain to break down an octopus in a cauldron that was cooking on a hotplate that stood halfway into the tiny little dining room.

Ⓐ 85 rue de la Roquette, 75011 Paris
Ⓣ +33 1 43 71 90 75

C B R 20 arr
Quartier Rouge
cafe, bar and restaurant

At this neighborhood pub I ate oysters for breakfast for the first time. We stepped in through the rickety glass doors to have a 1 euro coffee, and the bartender asked if we wanted to help him eat up the oysters that were left over from the night before. He was young with dark curly hair, and he conversed with me patiently in French while he opened the oysters, sniffed them, gave me the deep, cupped part and himself slurped the rest of the oyster from the shell. It is one of the best breakfasts I've eaten.

Sometimes there are concerts at Quartier Rouge, or used record sales and the worn wooden table fills with crates of vinyl records. People spill out onto the street and set down their glasses of Belgian beer on the roofs of parked cars so they can eat spicy mussels in oil from plastic takeaway containers, while arty-looking women sit at the bar and drink Japanese whiskey with lunch. Actually, not with lunch, but *for* lunch.

Everyone is welcome at Quartier Rouge: dogs and paupers, stressed office workers and e-cigarette smokers who go out, every day of the week, from nine in the morning to 2am at night. We are all treated with the same brisk friendliness. And, even more unique, lunch is served every day. Everything at Quartier Rouge feels like it's done with care, refined but humble and extremely affordable.

A 52 rue de Bagnolet, 75020 Paris
T +33 1 81 29 42 99

To the swamp!

Stolly's, 4 arr, bar
The same owners who run **Bottle Shop** (p. 117) also have the bar Stolly's, on the other side of Le Marais. Show up early to get a seat, and if you're hungry you can bring food with you into the outdoor seating area.

Stolly's is at times so popular that a bartender once decided to stop playing music. Instead he turned on the TV to a nature program and refused to serve people who hadn't brought their empty glasses back to the bar. Nothing helped. The bar continues to be packed, from graffitied stone wall to graffitied stone wall.

A 16 rue Cloche Percé, 75004 Paris
W cheapblonde.com
T +33 1 42 76 06 76

CAM, 3 arr, bar
The rowdy little restaurant Import/Export CAM is named as it is because that's what it originally said on the facade. Inside the door is a shelf with books about art and punk rock. In the kitchen are two young cooks who for a short time became stars, which didn't stop them from serving food when one of the waiters dropped a knife on their foot (true story). The price is low, atmosphere high and portions small. Sometimes you get your own plate, sometimes you share. The dishes contain only the best flavors from around the world. On Sundays tables fill with cooks from other fine bistros around Paris. Everyone speaks English.

A 55 Rue au Maire, 75003 Paris

Fine dining
and park life

The natural wine list at
Le Chateaubriand

Ⓡ 11 arr

Le Chateau-briand

restaurant

The late seating at Chateaubriand is like adventure tourism. Here's how it works. Sometimes it can be difficult to get a table at Chateaubriand, walk-ins show up instead at 9.30pm. This is the time you're told to show up, but in fact you should show up just after nine. Earlier than that, though, and you won't be let in. Once inside the gloomy space you will be trapped in a corral at the bar, along with as many other walk-ins as there's room for. Which is more than you'd imagine. Suck in your stomach. There we are then, everybody waiting nicely, until the early seating is finished. It can take a couple of hours. During which time, the staff are filling glass after glass of natural wine, while the corral grows more and more cramped as the typically late French people realize they are also hungry. But it's worth the wait.

Chateaubriand serves a set menu consisting of a large variety of dishes (was it 11 last time?!), which costs some ridiculously small amount in the range of 60–70 euro. You tell them in advance if you have any life-threatening allergies, and the cook decides the rest. Most of the dishes are twists, like for example a turnip that looks like a crabapple (carved and painted shiny bright-red, and when you look closely you realize the apple twig is actually a little dried fish) that tastes of fresh celery. It is foraged food that is actually good, at least most of the time. Sometimes it can be shocking. It's like keeping up with Charlie at a chocolate factory for adults. It's a place where the eyes and the tastebuds are constantly drawn into long, baffled discussions that often end with the mouth saying something along the lines of "Ah … umm … mmmm".

The staff are very French. Count on a scene if you dare to tell them you're that exotic type of vegetarian who doesn't eat any meat at all.

Ⓐ 129 avenue Parmentier, 75011 Paris
Ⓦ lechateaubriand.net
Ⓣ +33 1 43 57 45 95

R 11 arr

Le Dauphin

restaurant

Next to **Chateaubriand** (p. 139) is La
Cave, a store where they sell really nice
natural wines I can't afford, and next to La
Cave is Le Dauphin (The Crown Prince),
which is Chateaubriand's back pocket. Le
Dauphin serves equally fantastic ingredients
as Chateaubriand but without all the fuss.
Moreover it's easy to book a table, and if
you're early (which is to say not French) you
can slip in and get a seat at the bar.

The dishes are small: thin ceramic bowls of
Jerusalem artichoke soup, something avant-
garde from the sea, or just hand-picked leafy
greens and herbs. You don't have to share, but
you can.

A fantastic Colombian sommelier also works
here; once, after we closed Chateaubriand
together, she proved that she was a trained
ballet dancer by doing a perfect sissonne-and-
assemblé jump out into the street, along with
the broom she had just swept the floor with.

A 131 avenue Parmentier, 75011 Paris
W restaurantledauphin.net
T +33 1 55 28 78 88

R 19 arr

Mon Oncle le Vigneron

restaurant

Hang in there for one more special experience.
This little restaurant is on the way to **Parc
des Buttes-Chaumont (p. 142)** and the
experience is similar to that at **Chateaubriand**
(p. 139), if Chateaubriand had opened a branch
at the home of your French aunt and uncle in
the country.

You have to book a table – personally
I prefer to do it on-site, face to face, so I can fill
in my French with facial expressions and body
language. When you book, you should also say
whether you have allergies or are vegetarian,
and the rest is up to the cook.

Dinner is served in what looks like a
combination of a deli and a private kitchen,
where a happy woman cooks food for anyone
who comes to visit. The food is rustic, simple
and well-prepared, and the chef's husband
serves it. He also shows you photos of the pigs
the paté was made from.

The chairs and tables are mismatched,
the walls rough. Lined up on wine casks,
and tucked in among the potted plants in the
window, are small bottles of fiery strong but
dangerously good *eau de vie* made of plums,
pears or apples. They are small enough to
go into your luggage and a perfect present
for friends.

A 71 rue Rébeval, 75019 Paris
T +33 1 42 00 43 30

The Crown Prince's house

◎ 19 arr

Parc des Buttes-Chaumont
park
🐾🐾🐾

This is my, and every other park-lover's, favorite park in Paris. If it's full at **Parc de Belleville** (p. 158) there is usually a square meter free somewhere in Buttes-Chaumont, because it's so large that even after several years you can still get lost and find new hiding places.

Sometimes there's a tailgate flea market outside the park, and high up is the diner **Rosa Bonheur** where they sell coffee and wine in plastic cups. There's outdoor seating where you can eat cheese in the sun while chestnuts plonk down around you (sometimes they plonk so aggressively that there are warning signs on the trees). The diner also serves light dishes: tins of deli foods; a huge artichoke that keeps trying to roll off your paper plate, served only with a bowl of vinegar; fresh bread with a garlicky mishmash and other pickings.

The wifi password is the same as the name of the restaurant: rosabonheur. You will need it – the queue system is completely incomprehensible. You order certain drinks in an hour-long queue, and food and other drinks in a different equally long queue. It's the queue equivalent of Chinese water torture. I have stopped trying to figure out the system and these days content myself with either food or drink – whichever shows up at the end of the queue I'm standing in.

Parc des Buttes-Chaumont is also proof that landscape architects feel good about

a little grandeur. The view is laughably, breathtakingly Tolkien-esque.

Ⓐ 2 allée de la Cascade, 75019 Paris
Ⓦ rosabonheur.fr
Ⓣ +33 1 42 00 00 45

◎ Many arr

Ceinture railroad
railroad
🐾

One of the problems with democracy is that citizens are lulled into the belief that everything is perfect. That everything is already clear and fixed. It's this that makes people follow their GPS's driving instructions into rivers. It's the reason tourists desperate to pee who have lost their wallets tell the evening news that they never thought it could happen to them. That is also what makes democracies end up with dictators: we never thought something like this could happen to us. Again.

Thus, the following information I share as an anarchist. I'm counting on you to use it with full responsibility for your own life and safety. Ok?

So. There is an abandoned railway that winds its way through Paris like a sleepy, sun-drunk snake. It's called *Petite Ceinture* in French, and on Sundays, when the rest of the city is infested with rollerskaters and families with children, the Ceinture railroad is a great walking track. Especially if you are not afraid of rats and punks.

One place to get to the railroad is in **Parc des Buttes-Chaumont** (p. 142). When you stand with your back toward **Rosa Bonheur** take one of the paths to the right. Depending on which of the paths you choose you'll come either to a bridge over the train line, or arrive directly at it. It's fenced off in many places, but usually there's a fairly simple way in. There should be a fairly well-trodden path up to a more or less well-cut hole in the fence. It's worth taking time to seek out the best way in, so that you avoid tearing your clothes and the city of Paris avoids setting up another fence because another tourist climbed in at the wrong place. From Buttes-Chaumont the line goes into a tunnel, and on the other side of the tunnel it continues between high-rise buildings and over roads. It is a great spot from which to observe the city: at the height of the balconies. A good resting point is where Canal St-Martin runs out in the park La Villette. At the old arched bridge over the water it's possible to throw yourself down on the thick cross-ties that smell of creosote and eat a packed sandwich while you look down between the tracks at the crumbling repairs that look like they're waiting hungrily for a foot to slip down through the paper-thin, sharp metal.

The train lines can be enjoyed at a safe distance, also: you can sit outside the big glass windows at the concert venue La Flèche d'Or and look down at them, or see them from the outdoor-seating area at the luxury hotel Mama Shelter.

TIP

On rue Paul-Bert, where Bertrand Auboyneau has his little bistro empire, you can taste several of Paris' biggest food trends with only a few steps between them.

Bistro Paul Bert:
classic bistro/meat.
L'Ecailler du Bistrot:
classic bistro/fish.
Le 6 Paul Bert:
tapas and natural wine.
La Cave Du Paul Bert:
eat tapas in a natural wine cave

A 6–22 rue Paul-Bert, 75011 Paris

Outside the periphery

Earlier the **Ceinture railroad** (p. 142) was Paris' large ring-road. These days it's the motorway Périférique that rings the whole city and separates the inner-city's arrondissements from the suburbs. People usually cross the Périférique to do one of two things: go to a Congolese dancefest or shop at the super swish flea market at Clignancourt.

B 18 arr
La Recyclerie
bar

On the way to the flea market you inevitably pass La Recyclerie, yet another good place to enjoy the **Ceinture railroad** (p. 142) from, in a more or less orderly fashion. There are some problems with Recyclerie: prices (8 euro for a small beer), the type of hippies the place attracts (those who can pay 8 euro for beer, and still drink very many) and the lines. But as soon as someone puts a bar in an abandoned train station filled with exotic plants and lets chickens peck around in the outdoor seating area, you will, as a guest, immediately forget about all such problems.

A 83 boulevard Ornano, 75018 Paris
W larecyclerie.com
T +33 1 42 57 58 49

R 20 arr
Les Peres Populaires
restaurant

There is yet another known flea market outside the periphery, at Porte de Montreuil. If Clignancourt is expensive Danish design and museum objects, then Montreuil is used window treatments and old remote controls, but it's at least as fun an experience. It's a good bit of a walk to Montreuil, so be sure to make a pit stop at Les Peres Populaires. Many of the places in this book have reasonable prices, but no prices are as reasonable as those at Les Peres Populaires whose stated goals are to make everyday life extraordinary, for precisely everyone who is hungry or thirsty.

A 46 rue de Buzenval, 75020 Paris
T +33 1 43 48 49 22

Shall we go to Pigalle?

People tend to like Pigalle, which lies near Montmartre, Amelie's neighborhood and Sacre-Cœur. Caricature artists trawl the streets, drunk tourists listen to "jazz" at outdoor tables and police with sharp weapons chase aggressive street vendors. To me Pigalle is totally incomprehensible. In addition to the decadence, which feels museum-like, Pigalle is all about expensive pizzerias, cocktail bars and brunch places where people in expensive raglan cardigans carry around fat babies in expensive baby slings.

There is, however, a small isolated bar-island in Pigalle, where people who work in bars in the 11th go when everything else is closed: **Glass**, **Pigalle Country Club**, **Lulu White** and especially **Dirty Dick** (mostly, I suspect, because they all worked there once and still get an employee discount).

If I am in Pigalle I usually go to **La Fourmi** and eat crispy French fries at a rickety table, under the enormous bottle-drying rack that hangs from the roof. Or I'll drink beer at **Bar Rock n Roll Circus**, which is actually nice and not in that uncertain way, like most cocktail bars. It is worn-in and warm, and the last time I was here nobody on the staff had a sweater on.

But the very best thing about Pigalle is still that you can leave and go back to the 11th. Like the time when we left a party and were on the way home through the cold, wet, quiet night, euphoric and loudly chattering like kids ditching school. We were not even halfway home when a drunk Frenchman zigzag-cycled toward us on the street. He stopped and asked, in French, if we knew the way to République, Bastille or Gare d'Austerlitz. We laughed, because that is three totally different places, which all lie around 20 minutes from each other. I answered in French, "République is nearby, just take Magenta straight ahead". The Frenchman got off his cycle and walked toward us: "Are you Belgians?" No, Swedes. The Frenchman took another step toward us, his expression had changed and he continued in English, "So you come here, to my country, my home, and give me instructions on how I should get home?! Fuck Le Pen! This is my welcome! This night I'll tell stories about!"

He threw himself onto his bike, quickly picked up speed, zigzagged on down along Magenta laughing happily while he waved back at us in a slightly dangerous way.

Dirty Dick, 9 arr, cocktail bar
Ⓐ 10 rue Frochot, 75009 Paris
Ⓣ +33 1 48 78 74 58

La Fourmi, 18 arr, bar and restaurant
Ⓐ 74 rue des Martyrs, 75018 Paris
Ⓣ +33 1 42 64 70 35

Bar Rock n Roll Circus, 18 arr, bar
Ⓐ 5 rue André Antoine, 75018 Paris
Ⓣ +33 6 09 81 93 59

Rue Saint-Maur, northward & beyond

◎ 20 arr

Cimetière du Père-Lachaise

cemetery

🐾🐾🐾

People will tell you it's cheesy to go to Père-Lachaise cemetery. This is not true and everyone who says that needs to get new glasses. Père-Lachaise is one of the prettiest places in Paris. Winding paths lead to a confusing tangle of dilapidated graves. Bare-breasted mourners throw themselves in despair over rough-hewn graves. Huge ravens shriek menacingly from the tops of bare trees draped with evergreen mistletoe.

When the end-of-year frost covers the whole cemetery, when all the plants' shady sides seem to be powdered with ancient dust and when the cold from the stone walkways goes right through the soles of your shoes and into the bone marrow, the beauty is so overwhelming that it feels like a physical presence. The soul sings and the eyes tear up. Here I have performed rituals and lost myself in gothic fantasies. But usually I go here just to try to read the secret messages in the plants. Mistletoe – a terrible parasite that grows without ever touching the ground – hangs directly over thorny holly, the underworld plant that has been planted in cemeteries to give unsavory spirits a door back to the underground. Large yews – the druids' holy tree which can be over 1,000 years old – are framed by ivy in large black bracelets. In the same way, the ivy has grown on the church walls and around gravesites ever since pre-Christian times.

I also go to Père-Lachaise to look at people looking at Jim Morrison's grave. The musician Geoff was born and raised in a suburb of Paris and when he was little his father took him along to just this grave. This was the '80s, when people still hung out around gravestones, listening to music, drinking and joking around. Geoff doesn't say so himself, but it seems likely that it was there and then that he decided that he too should become a rock star when he grew up. For a long time the tree at the gravesite was so full of teenagers' chewing gum that the whole place smelled like strawberry and peppermint. Nowadays the grave has a fence around it and the tree has a protective bamboo jacket that is replaced periodically. But it's still one of the finest parts of the cemetery.

Another fun grave for tourists is Oscar Wilde's large stone. It is now glassed-in because the porous, light stone was weathered and crumbling from all the lipstick of the people who kissed it.

There are more obscure graves also. Like those that Mike visits. Mike is an English immigrant bartender and author, and he has been so often to Père-Lachaise that the cemetery finally offered him a job as a guide. On Mike's tour, if it had existed, you would

follow along to the gravestone marked with only a single word: Sextoy*. But you would also be led to the mausoleum where there lies a woman who left behind her a challenge to those who outlived her: to spend the nights down there in the dark with her. Those who can handle it become the legal heir to her fortune. According to legend, all who have tried have died or lost their minds.

* Sextoy's real name was Delphine Palatsi, she was a groundbreaking French DJ and died of a heart attack in 2002.

Ⓐ One entrance is at 16 rue du Repos, 75020 Paris

Ⓦ parisinfo.com/musee-monument-paris/71470/Cimetiere-du-Pere-Lachaise

Ⓣ +33 1 55 25 82 10

R 11 arr

Le Servan
restaurant

When the two sisters who run Le Servan bought a place at the intersection of rue Saint-Maur and rue du Chemin Vert, right across the street from the anarchist bar **In The Garden** (p. 156), there was already a restaurant running in the space. The building is old, the roof in the place was obviously sinking and the walls were dull. They decided to tear everything down and start from the beginning. And because they peeled back layer after layer of modern renovations they discovered the treasure that is now Le Servan. Weirdly detailed stucco that resembles fluffy, freshly spread cream; tall, coarse pillars with the worn residue of Tiffany-blue wall murals; a well-preserved ceiling painting that looks like an impressionist dream (if you like impressionism, which you realize you do as soon as you come into Le Servan). In the blue sky on the ceiling, one swallow flies in either direction. The sisters have tried to find out why the place looks the way it does, but no one in the building – not even the old concierge – remembers what was here in the beginning. The best guess is that maybe it was a highbrow bakery once, a long time ago, before rue Saint-Maur filled up with dive bars and natural-wine restaurants.

There under the swallows I have eaten a whole meal consisting solely of mollusks: a bucket of whelks, served naked as Gaia made them, with a little bowl of herb mayonnaise by its side and a snail needle, which is used to pry out the snails from their shells. After that, tiny little cockles with broth and chilies,

followed by grilled scallops served with sweet, caramelized endive and filleted clementine wedges. Tatiana Levha also does something totally fantastic with vegetables and tempura. Like a bowl of baby artichokes, so delicate that you could eat them whole, covered with a cloud-like fluffy batter. At first you're a little disappointed. Where is the dip? Are we savages or what?! Then you take a bite and realize that some maniac hid the dip in the little heads before they were fried. There are also more adventuresome, meaty things: the highly loved French blood sausage and something described as cow's face. Do you mean cheek? "No, face." Do you mean … brains? "No", (a circling gesture around the face), "face". Cow's face is served in the form of a little hamburger, with paper-thin bread, and is very oily.

Unlike many other natural-wine places that serve only tapas plates, you can choose yourself what type of dinner you want to have at Le Servan: either a mishmash of small plates and starters, or a traditional three-course meal. There's usually some vegetarian dish on the menu, and vegetables in tempura vary by the season: artichokes are followed by asparagus, which are followed by chicory. The only thing I haven't fallen for are the desserts. Everything else at Le Servan is simple but delicious, with 100 times more flavor than at ordinary French restaurants, and comparatively cheap and unpretentious despite the difficult words on the menu.

A 32 rue Saint-Maur, 75011 Paris
W leservan.com
T +33 1 55 28 51 82

Multi-tasking griddle

Ⓡ 11 arr

Achille :'(
restaurant
👣 👣 👣

The first time we noticed Svante Forstorp was when he was pattering around at **Aux Deux Amis** (p. 28) with his ultra careful aura. There he served all the things people love, in a tiny little dish, without anyone making a big deal about how perfect it was. After that he showed up at the legendary natural-wine restaurant **Vivant** (p. 155). When Achille finally opened Svante had already become a star.

In this little tiny place Svante works in an open kitchen, while Pierre Jancou, in an obligatory rough-knit sweater (alias natural-wine jacket), takes care of the floor along with Justine. To eat at Achille feels very much like going to a friend's house for dinner. If those friends just happened to prepare jaw-dropping food and serve wine made by their friends, who happen to be France's best wine producers. None of this, of course, is a coincidence, but the atmosphere is so free and easy that you might well begin to spontaneously enjoy it before you start to appreciate the enormous effort and experience behind it. Doing something difficult with ease is also at least twice as hard as doing it with a sweaty brow and white knuckles.

We have to start by talking about the oysters. The dish is like a little story. The oysters are served with their tops on, and (spoiler alert!) feel hot against the fingertips when you curiously touch them to find out if this can really mean that you're supposed to open your own oysters in a restaurant. Then, when you've plucked off the top with

no problem, it turns out to be deconstructed oysters Rockefeller, meltingly good with baked breadcrumbs and leeks. They also serve a large bowl of thick broth, with a spoon for each person around the table, and something disguised as beef tartare. Once it was a clever imitation of raw beef that tasted tartly of mixed citrus. Another time the raw beef was made of layer after layer of the year's first asparagus: boiled green under a blanket of smoked white. Everything is whimsical and surprising, both extravagant and simple, and laced with quiet humor. To serve a small plate with a lot of well prepared, beautiful spaghetti seems almost absurd. Like, "What do you mean? Spaghetti is good, we serve good things". Many times we have, in a dictatorial way, commanded our dinner company to order the spaghetti. Afterwards all of them have agreed that it was one of the best dishes ("How can it be so good? It's just spaghetti!"). When I told this to Svante he replied, "We want to bring back the opportunity to be pleasantly surprised. It is so often the opposite these days, don't you think?" I was touched.

You can keep picking at small things until your stomach is full and you've drunk all the natural wine in the world that has a bottle cap (like the good, pink, juicy Festejar). Or you can take a stab at a monster fish that's served whole, with all its body parts intact, on a large, ornate, slightly dented metal dish that tips slightly when each person takes their portion. I think that it is like eating Friday dinner at the home of one of those women who know both how to strangle doves and how to get rid of bloodstains with the help of soda water, ammonia and a little diesel. Or something.

This is one of the places I never stop dreaming about, even when I'm not in Paris. To eat at Achille is a careful, ethereal experience. I was struck only afterward, when it had all sunk in. Like when I realized that they didn't use any machines in the minimalist kitchen – because that would disturb the diners. The last machine was a hand-mixer that gave Svante a shock and blew out all the lights in the place. After that he decided that there was enough electricity in the world and got himself a man-size mortar and pestle instead. There he grinds yesterday's leftover bread for tomorrow's baked oysters. The mood in the kitchen is also decided by the size of the place. The classic angry chef won't work. The movements are careful, almost ritualistic. Svante says that this is not something you

can turn on and off; the same respect and care must be taken through the whole process. This begins as soon as the goods arrive: to stack each sea urchin in a pretty way in the fridge instead of just throwing them in. When I say that it sounds like a tea ceremony, but with lots of wine, Svante nods silently but enthusiastically.

The bread comes from Alice Quillet at **10 Belles Bread**, and like all the rest is delicious. More often than not James Henry sits in the bar, the chef who started **Bones** (**Jones**, p. 18) and who has a half-manic fan following. These days he bakes bread along with Alice while he fixes up a biodynamic farm outside Paris.

The last time I spoke with Svante was right after I finished writing this book, and he told me Achille would close. A neighbor had reported the noise level and they had two options: soundproofing for an astronomical sum and, even worse, cover up the magnificent

ceiling fixture. Or hold themselves to the same rules as any tenant: no to-do after ten. Pierre Jancou, along with some of the staff, continued with his own project **Ground Control**, at Gare de Lyon. Svante himself has only a pair of servings left and says it feels like a graduation. "This was a performance even from the beginning. We knew it when we opened. We named the restaurant Achille. You know the legend: you can drag out the war, you know what you've come to do, but you know that you'll leave a legacy."

A ~~43 rue Servan, 75011 Paris~~
T ~~+33 1 48 06 54 59~~

TIP

Vivant
10 arr, restaurant

Pierre Jancou is a natural wine extremist and his cave Vivant cemented the tradition of eating tapas at natural-wine caves in Paris. These days, though, Vivant has new owners.

A **43 rue des Petites Écuries, 75010 Paris**
W **vivantparis.com**
T **+33 1 42 46 43 55**

OYSTERS À LA SVANTE
Serves 4

"Oysters have to do with childhood memories: like remembering an involuntary gulp of cold water from when you were ten and swimming and tried to sidestep a jellyfish or something. They are special to serve also. They are alive, you are facing something that's alive, and the oyster doesn't need a touch of anything else before you hand it over. What could be more special?

Oysters also have a longer shelf life than many think, like ten days. Up to 14, but let's say ten for safety's sake. Some compare oysters with aged red meat: that the taste matures with time. Those last three days perhaps they begin to get a little dry and slimy, but until then they just get better and more flavorful."

5½ oz (75 g) butter
⅓ leek
salt to taste
half a baguette (preferably 1-day old)
4 oysters of medium size, apr. no 3
½ lemon, zest and juice

Melt the butter over medium heat, until it's golden-brown and frothy, about ten minutes – you are looking for a nutty tone in the aroma.

Shred the leek, including some of the green part, as thinly as you can. Place the leek in the butter, add salt and cook on a low heat until the leeks are tender and have soaked up all the butter, 15–20 minutes depending on how finely cut they are.

Toast the bread in the oven and crush it into breadcrumbs with a rolling pin.

Remove the leeks from the heat and mix in the breadcrumbs. Let's say one part breadcrumbs to two parts leek. Add pepper to taste and finish with finely grated lemon zest and juice to desired tartness.

Open the oysters, cut off the muscle and pull away any debris. Spread the breadcrumb mix over the oysters, approximately 1 tablespoon each depending on size.

I bake the oysters in a salamander, a type of sandwich grill, but high oven temperatures and the grill setting should give a similar effect. Bake the oysters high up in the oven, until the breadcrumbs turn golden brown – it only takes a minute or two. Serve immediately.

In The Garden
bar

It was an early evening in January, the day after Chelsea Manning's release was announced. My cellphone thought it was minus 3 degrees Celsius out (27 degrees Fahrenheit), but the "real feel" was minus 10 (14 degrees Fahrenheit), and people were dying of the cold in Poland. We chose to slip into In The Garden mostly because we couldn't manage to go any farther from home. We each drank room-temperature (therefore ice-cold) pints with jackets and beanies on. A tiny computer played a tinny version of Joy Division's ice-cold *Warsaw*. The table was covered with pages torn from a comic book and the walls around the bar were covered with stickers – Lemmy Kilmister, Ace of Spades, slogans like "*ni dieu, ni maître*" (no gods, no masters) and, more confusingly, "We aren't here to sell cod". Farthest back in the place was the bar's only heating element; I went to the restroom mostly so I could pass by it. In the restroom it was even colder and on the walls was just one sticker: "Free Chelsea Manning". I half-stood and cheered inside over being right there, right then, at maybe the only moment in world history when an American president used his power to fulfill a little anarchist French bar's impossible wish that a freedom fighter, sentenced to nearly 40 years in jail, be released. And everything in the world was right and soft and warm. Then I slipped a little, hit the seat and it felt like sitting on ice again.

A super fun thing about this type of bar is that they won't have anything to do with big business. Therefore all the beer at In The Garden is handcrafted. There are masses of nerdy bottles to choose from, but the prices are still totally ok. I have so far never heard a bad song here and the atmosphere is often tops.

A 39 rue Saint-Maur, 75011 Paris
T +33 9 52 68 20 02

Le Zingam
food shop

Le Zingam is approximately the same thing as the farmers market–shop **Maison POS** (p. 113), but in a different area. Exactly as it must be, if everyone is to be able to shop for inexpensive, locally produced, eco-friendly food. And because farmers differ, the stores that sell direct from farmers are also different.

At Le Zingam I can buy insanely good burrata for only 5 euro. It is the absolute freshest and explodes in an eruption of cream when you set a knife to it. The shop also sells large chunks of brie and small tins of honey. If you're here, look extra carefully for the anonymous white plastic tubs with the misleading name "*crème fraiche crue*" written on a label. *Crème fraiche* isn't fresh cream, but ripe cream. *Crue* means raw. So this is a thick, unpasteurized, aged cream in a container. In the US it would be illegal to sell.

The cream comes from sweet, brown-spotted Normandy cows who look as if they're wearing glasses. The cows are allowed to graze and their ripe, raw cream is sticky, ivory-colored, pale and very thick. The flavor is mild and barely sour at all. It has wild, earthy undertones and so much fat that the tongue feels buttery after you've eaten it. Drop the cream over a little Bonne Maman chocolate mousse that you've bought at the corner store, or use it in a black-radish salad. Make the salad by mixing 1 part lemon, 1 part Dijon mustard and 2 parts cream. Pour the mixture over sliced black radish, let it stand for a few hours, then eat it with a fork, by the mouthful, directly out of the mixing bowl.

Here you also see pretty often the owner-chef of **La Buvette** (p. 158), the tiny little natural-wine restaurant that lies just up on rue Saint-Maur.

Ⓐ 75 rue du Chemin Vert, 75011 Paris
Ⓦ lezingam.com
Ⓣ +33 7 87 55 65 56

Ⓞ 11 arr

Variations Végétales
flower shop

Just a few blocks below rue Saint-Maur is the little park-like Square Maurice Gardette, where the concentration of pleasant nonsense is extra high. Here, among other things, is the little flower shop Variations Végétales.

Anthroposophists aren't always the world's easiest to do business with, every god knows, but cultivation – that they can do. And without knowing anything about this cultivating florist's view of life, her tiny little shop certainly feels anthroposophist. Here are little herbs and potted plants, but the very best thing at Variations Végétales are the cut flowers that stand gathered in rough armfuls. Everything is simple, locally grown and country-style (for reals, not the way people in The Hamptons mean it). They also sell sprawling, bare twigs during winter and decadent swaying tulips in spring. Here you'll find everything for your ikebana needs and absolutely nothing else.

Ⓐ 18 rue du Général Guilhem, 75011 Paris
Ⓦ variationsvegetales.com
Ⓣ +33 1 43 55 22 45

(R) (ws) 11 arr

La Buvette
restaurant and wine shop

Camille Fourmant worked as the bar manager at **Le Dauphin** (p. 140) before she opened the micro-restaurant La Buvette in a former dairy shop (hence the name), where she now serves tapas and natural wines. The place consists of little more than two tables, and Camille's rockstar status means you sometimes must fight hard to get a seat at them. When you luck out you can snack on cold cuts and antipasti, and drink Camille's well chosen wines. La Buvette is a wine cave also, and it works equally well to buy wine to take home.

(A) 67 rue Saint-Maur, 75011 Paris
(T) +33 9 83 56 94 11

(O) 20 arr

Parc de Belleville
park

After you've stopped in for a glass at **La Buvette** (p. 158), you can continue northward along rue Saint-Maur, all the way to rue de la Fontaine au Roi. There you'll swing off to the right. After a few blocks you pass into the 20th arrondissement and then gradually Parc de Belleville turns up. It is a small, heavily terraced park with very fine bamboo. From above it looks like a web woven by a drunk spider. I like to ascend the park – from below and up is best – and fantasize about how it would have been to play war here when you were little. Way up at the top of the park there's one of the best views in all of Paris. It easily beats the Sacré-Cœur view, and besides I prefer the vendors in Parc de Belleville.

There's a small wine bar at the crest of the park, and if the sun is shining, it's tempting to stop and have a glass here. Don't do it. If you want a drink with the view it's better to buy a bottle to bring with you. Takeaway coffee is an unknown invention around the 11th and 20th*, but there's always wine. And maybe a *pain au chocolat*?

Parc de Belleville is also a good way to enjoy the Eiffel Tower, without the need to go to the terrible area where the tower stands. Sunset is beyond perfect.

* The only ones who drink takeaway coffee are construction workers. Early in the morning you can see them stand and smoke beside their backhoes – big dusty fists that hold vanishingly tiny mugs, filled with at most two centimeters of coffee.

Ⓐ **47 rue des Couronnes, 75020 Paris**
Ⓣ **+33 1 43 15 20 20**

Ⓡ 20 arr

Le Jourdain
restaurant

If you ignore the two uppity places that fight for people just at the crest of **Parc de Belleville** (p. 158), continue along rue de Transvaal and then swing up to the left, Le Jourdain is there and eagerly waiting, framed by remarkable street art, vacant lots and shops that sell art supplies. At lunch the sun falls in between the buildings on the small outdoor-seating area, and at night you can squeeze in to the small place with its bare walls, and eat a bit of food on coarse, handmade crockery.

Everything served here is genuinely homemade, all the produce is cut by hand and the plates composed according to the chef's specific taste. The young waiters look like any of the other scrawny guys in the neighborhood, those who hang around in little gangs with entirely too large scooters. With the difference being that they look at you curiously, rather than suspiciously. When two friends turned up at Le Jourdain directly from their flight, with their things in two suitcases, the waiter threw the suitcases up on his back and disappeared with them down through a dangerous hole in the floor. Another time, when I hesitated a few seconds between French fries and bean salad as a side to my main course, he decided in a flash that I should have both. When I asked if the fresh, white wine we drank was organic he lashed out with his teenager's hands and said, "No, it actually contains a little trace of sulfur. But only to stabilize it." Organic enough for me, clearly.

Le Jourdain is civilized, honest, rough and pretty at the same time – like the dream of the perfect neighborhood bistro, come true. And the portions and the prices are such that you actually can manage to eat a three-course meal for lunch even if you aren't normally a three-course-lunch kind of person.

Ⓐ **101 rue des Couronnes, 75020 Paris**
Ⓦ **restaurantlejourdain.com**
Ⓣ **+33 1 43 66 29 10**

R 20 arr

Le Baratin
restaurant

Le Baratin is a very classic place that has been here, in Belleville, for more than 30 years. Owner-chef Raquel Carena bought the abandoned bistro for "nothing", so that her boyfriend would have a place to serve natural wine. This kitchen is the first one she's cooked in.

Baratin is one of those places that has earned diners' trust. But it also has a reputation for unfriendly service. I have never noticed any of that. On the contrary. To visit Baratin is an old-fashioned experience. It feels like eating from Alice B Toklas' cookbook. There's a three-course lunch for the extremely reasonable price of 19 euro, and each dish, each ingredient, has clearly been touched by a human hand. Each sea snail is carefully chopped, each sturdy piece of fish is cut with a determination that is felt as much as seen. It is heartfelt food, well made, without apologies. One white wine, Stéphane Bernaudeau's Les Onglés, which is dry and flavorful, is served with an apple crumble that makes me think of childhood pies I never ate.

I also love restaurants where the cook actually stands in the kitchen. Like when we came early for lunch (12.15pm is basically a builders' lunch in Paris) and Raquel looked up with a quick, tight smile, so she could continue to write the day's menu on a slate.

A 3 rue Jouye-Rouve, 75020 Paris
T +33 1 43 49 39 70

B 20 arr

Aux Folies
bar

Aux Folies' huge outdoor-seating area is chock-full year-round, every day of the week, for the better part of the day. One time the bar opened at 5.30am. It may sound early, but it isn't. In actual fact it was late: you could go here to eat breakfast when the bars that closed very last finally threw everyone out again.

It can be tempting to describe Aux Folies' outdoor seating as a place where you sit in order to see and be seen. But this is both an unkind way to describe a place and, besides, totally wrong. Nowhere in the conglomeration of people who balance on the rickety chairs is there anyone who's interested in checking anyone out. Street vendors who offer up mysterious Chinese vegetables and little old ladies who sell things from canvases on the sidewalk have no interest in looking at you either. The smartly dressed prostitutes don't care, and the teenagers who hang out at the red light and drink bubble tea with soy milk couldn't care less. The people you sit shoulder-to-shoulder with nod without looking up when you accidentally bump them with your arm. Aux Folies is a place where you go to be alone in a crowd, to drink a small glass of cold tart wine. You go here to meet no one you know. Not to disappear, exactly, but to show up, without a trace.

A 8 rue de Belleville, 75020 Paris
W aux-folies-belleville.fr
T +33 6 28 55 89 40

⊙ 20 arr

Rue Dénoyez

street

🔲

In Paris there are two things that are missing in many other modern capital cities: new buildings constructed in classic style and graffiti. I don't really know how the two hang together, but they do. Perhaps they are two different expressions of humanism? Who knows?

Rue Dénoyez, aka Graffiti Street, disappears around the corner from **Aux Folies** (p. 160), and often you can smell the paint thinner all the way to the outdoor seating. It is like a sweet perfume for all who live where all the newly built houses have facades in glass and other easily cleaned materials.

The street is mainly about the most life-affirming form of graffiti, pure vandalism, where the action, not the result, is the important thing. It is a living, changing artwork, which meets and spreads out in waves, night after night.

Here is a good thing to meditate on when you walk along rue Dénoyez: that the city never became a complete utopia and that the dream of modernism therefore is false. A city is a living organism, an unwritten framework that constantly has to negotiate and renegotiate based on all the people, needs and expressions that crowd that particular place. When I think about this I usually get so faint with hunger that I must immediately go to **Le Grand Bain** (p. 163).

Ⓐ rue Dénoyez, 75020

Le Grand Bain

restaurant

It's not weird that it was here on **rue Dénoyez** (p. 162) that Edward Delling-Williams decided to open his own restaurant, after he had left **Au Passage** (p. 10). It seems obvious that he should be on a street that buzzes with both thoughtfulness and tear-up-the-old energy. And while Au Passage lives on, as viable as ever, yet another small piece of Au Passage has sprung up and made yet another part of the city a little better.

Le Grand Bain had already achieved credibility, very soon after the place opened at the end of 2016. I can't remember there being anything that even resembled a restaurant here before. The menu cares very little about what anyone else thinks. The dishes are written on a pane of glass near the kitchen. Numbers that slowly tick down to zero in front of the more exclusive dishes show when the food runs out. Which is both fun, exciting and symbolic in a way: things run out; food gets eaten up. I read once that the reason many Parisian restaurants only serve fixed-price menus* or *carte blanche*** is that Parisians have a tendency to sit long and eat little. The idea with dishes that run out seems more fun: it becomes like a game to compose the dinner you want to have.

* A set number of dishes for a set price.
** You're told what the meal will cost, but don't ask any questions beyond that, just accept what you're served.

The first time we went to Grand Bain I became alarmed when we ordered *chou rouge* (red cabbage) and what showed up on the table was a plate full of … red cabbage. I had assumed that *chou rouge* was a fun euphemism for something more exotic. The red cabbage even smelled Swedish-Asian: bay leaf and allspice and, well, cabbage. But on top of the red cabbage was a mountain of ricotta, among which hid fresh tarragon leaves, and the whole dish was sprinkled with fried onions. I love fried onions. I ventured a bite. The cabbage was creamy, fatty and with a perfect umami flavor, the tarragon tasted of licorice and the ricotta was fresh. To claim that it was the best red cabbage I've ever eaten isn't saying much. But I'll say this: the chance of any other red cabbage out there to live up to my new expectations is now infinitesimal. As other dishes showed up I began to smile. It is a joke, it is Food without Borders, a refusal to accept that certain things that come from certain places must never meet other things that come from other places. The table filled with small plates. A tiny little bit of raw shark, Japanese and simple. Four balls of fried brie with cranberry jam to dip them in – they sounded Czech, but tasted like cheese poppers at some British pub that only exists in my dreams. A piece of octopus tentacle stood like a rigid garland up from a dish filled with little Chinese mustard leaves. A bowl of walnuts, both sweet and salty in that way Americans love.

The menu changes from visit to visit. Once, all it said was "PDT" along the bottom of the glass pane. PDT is the abbreviation for potatoes and if potatoes are on the menu, you must order potatoes. It turned out to be a sort of combination of the classic French dish *pommes anna* and a *mille-feuille* pastry.

The potatoes were sheer-sliced, placed in layers (it's a good guess that there was butter involved in the game), baked like a cake, chopped up in thick slabs and fried. The result was a very baroque interpretation of giant French fries.

The food at Grand Bain is quick and varied. You won't necessarily like everything. But before you can get too hung up on anything, another little bowl shows up on the table, something new and exciting for 6–7 euro, and then you go out into the world again. With everything, they serve French sourdough bread baked in-house – presumably in the mixer that Edward was aimlessly carrying around the place one time when we arrived early – from flour that's ground in a little kitchen grinder, from grain produced by a farmer who Edward name-checks in interviews.

For dessert there's often a dish called *île flottante* (floating island). It's a piece of half-baked meringue, the same kind you find atop baked Bombe Alaska or inside coconut cups. The meringue floats in a little sea of sweet sauce made from egg yolk. Yet another dessert that is too French for me. I prefer the deconstructed pear-crumble pie, consisting solely of a naked, baked pear that itself tastes of caramel, a hefty load of loosely whipped cream and crumbly pie topping. In other words, exactly the ingredients you want in a crumble.

Ⓐ 14 rue Denoyez, 75020 Paris
Ⓦ legrandbainparis.com
Ⓣ +33 9 83 02 72 02

Edouard.

Edward.

Q/A
Where do you eat?
Edward Delling-Williams

Along with people like James Henry, Quina Lon (p. 41) and Peter Orr (p. 23), Edward is a co-creator of the new French market-based cooking. When they started at Au Passage (p. 10) they were all still youngsters. Now Edward – an immigrant from southeast England – has the power and ability to change

Parisians' itineraries, having opened his own restaurant on a back street. Edward lives in the 18th arrondissement with his wife and small child, but still seems to have – at least – as much energy as before.

Do you have a signature dish?
Bombe Alaska with coconut flavor.

What do you listen to while you work?
Everything! Starting with Nick Cave and going all the way to Madonna, depending on how fast I want people to work.

Do you have any favorite ingredients?
Mussels. Or whatever people usually throw away, like broccoli stalks for example.

Are you a regular at any restaurants?
Ravioli Nord-Est! or **Deux Fois Plus de Piment**
(p. 52).

Where do you go to drink?
Aux Folies (p. 160), or the scruffy dive bars near
where I live in the 18th. I love that area.

When you tasted natural wine for the first time,
where were you and what did you think?
2012, when I came to Paris and Au Passage.
I thought it was super — new, refreshing, exciting!

What's the best dinner you've eaten in Paris?
Christmas Eve dinner with my then pregnant wife
at Deux Fois Plus de Piment — that is my best
dinner experience. Best meal purely in terms of
food: either **Chateaubriand** (p. 139) or **Clown
Bar** (p. 32).

Do you have a magical flavor combo,
something that you invented yourself,
inherited or were served by someone else?
XO sauce with octopus!

Where do you eat?

Edouard Lax

Edward's partner at Grand Bain (p. 163) is
named, confusingly enough, Edouard. He
was born and raised in Paris, and lives in
the 18th arrondissement. At Grand Bain
he manages the hectic floor, recognizes
everyone he's ever met, and puts together
the dangerously cheap natural-wine list, where
he often sneaks in some more obscure pearls
that people who follow wine usually become
obsessed with.

What's your favorite wine right now?
Geschickt, Alsace Riesling 2014 Kaefferkopf.

What do you listen to while you work?
Anderson Paak.

What is your favorite dish at Le Grand Bain?
Mussels, cauliflower, miso.

Are you a regular at any restaurants?
WenZhou (p. 76) in Belleville.

Where do you drink?
At home!

When you tasted natural wine for the first time,
where were you and what did you think?
L'Entrée des Artistes, 2013. I thought, hmm … I
must learn more about this.

What's the best dinner you've eaten in Paris?
Clown Bar (page 32).

Do you have a magical flavor combo,
something that you invented yourself,
inherited or were served by someone else?
Chocolate mousse, salt and olive oil with a
glass of sweet red wine, like Brin de Folie from
Domaine de Brin.

Beyond food
and drink

Various arrondissements

Tabio 4 arr, shop

Paris is a specialized city. You buy bread at the bakery, meat at the butcher, produce at the market and socks at the sock store. It's not that Paris is extra-obsessed with socks. I have only seen one sock store, this one, and it consists of only one room. But in this room there are only socks. All kinds of socks. Totally ordinary black socks. Socks in every color. Socks for men, women and children. Socks without elastic for people with sensitive ankles. Super-glittery socks, semi-glittery socks and just barely glittery socks. In every color. For men and women. Socks in all sizes. And by that I mean not just sizes of feet, but also the socks' height on the leg. There are thigh-high socks and then every possible length from there down, from knee socks and ankle socks to sports socks. There is one sock for only the front half of the foot and one for only the heel. There's a sock only for the toes (not like those disagreeable "gloves" for the feet, but toe socks that look exactly like normal socks except they cover only the toes). There is a sock exclusively for the big toe. The very smallest sock I have seen here is a sock exclusively for the gaps between the toes; like a crocheted knuckle-duster for the foot. You haven't lived until you've lived in a city where they sell socks – in many different colors – exclusively for the gaps between the toes. All existence before this is just waiting, surviving, not a real and fulfilling life.

(A) **15 rue Vieille du Temple, 75004 Paris**
(W) **tabio.fr**
(T) **+33 1 42 78 20 38**

Odetta 3 arr, shop

Odetta is a little vintage store with well-chosen clothing, jewelry and furniture. But primarily they sell a special type of cowboy boots from Camargue, made by the last French cowboy-boot factory. They are low boots in suede, also known as "rock moccasins", with a soft strip that stretches down around the foot. If you dare to get them resoled they'll last half a lifetime and get trendier every year.

The guy who runs the store is a little gruff. Lately he has seemed to be tired of customers, and these days he locks the door from inside. If you knock, he'll open it. Sometimes. When I said that I was thinking of resoling my rock moccasins, he made a face like a squirrel trying to get loose a wafer stuck to the roof of its mouth.

(A) **76 rue des Tournelles, 75003 Paris**
(W) **odettavintage.com**
(T) **+33 1 48 87 08 61**

Doursoux 11 arr, shop

Here you'll find fine military surplus clothes and antique soldier stuff. It lies in Doursoux on rue Amelot, near **Clown Bar** (p. 32), but the one at 3 Passage Alexandre in the 15th arrondissement is almost better. I go here to buy knives, watches and thick military sweaters.

One tip. Shop here on your first day in Paris, save the receipt and double-check that the watches, lighters and such actually work. The things they sell are sometimes a little wonky, but so long as you have time and a handwritten receipt it's no problem to exchange them.

(A) **131 rue Amelot, 75011 Paris**
(W) **doursoux.com**
(T) **+33 1 47 00 01 82**

OFR 3 arr, shop

Everyone calls this place O-F-R, but it's actually called Zero Franc – no money – because the owners had that much money when they started the shop. It's a really well organized newsstand which sells international newspapers and magazines and also sells some handmade porcelain and a bunch of style- and art books.

(A) **20 rue Dupetit-Thouars, 75003 Paris**
(T) **+33 1 42 45 72 88**

The Abbey Bookshop

5 arr, shop

One of the world's best known bookshops is Shakespeare & Co, where Ernest Hemingway used to hang out (his typewriter is still there, upstairs). Paris' oldest tree grew up right outside, and the previous owner used to cut his hair by burning it. Nothing against Shakespeare & Co, but it's a little like going to Stockholm's Old Town when you need a new Viking helmet. But if I actually want to buy a book in English, I go to Abbey Books.

- **A** 29 rue de la Parche-minerie, 75005 Paris
- **W** abbeybookshop.wordpress. com
- **T** +33 1 46 33 16 24

Un Regard Moderne
6 arr, shop
This tiny little bookstore is run by an obvious hoarder. There are lots of comics, one part smut and a hint of occultism. It's no use being shy: it is impossible to find anything yourself, so you must say what you're looking for to the man slinking around the book labyrinth, whereupon he coaxes out the books like a master of pick-up-sticks from the bottom of a dangerously high stack.

- **A** 10 rue Gît-le-Cœur, 75006 Paris
- **T** +33 1 43 29 13 93

Le Cabinet du Dr Stendahl
20 arr (Montrouge), squat
Le Stendahl is a squat (aka an occupied building) and once a week it invites the whole neighborhood in for a party, under the name "*Jeudi du Chaos*" (Thursday's chaos). Here various DJs play such loud music that I have seen the plaster in the ceiling crumble and a spotlight fall

down and hang by its cord. Someone told me the genre they play is speedcore, and I certainly wouldn't say that it's bad. But not good, either. It lives instead in that large and crowded musical landscape of "interesting but unlistenable".

Everything at Le Stendahl is *prix libre* (priced by donation): admission, books, fanzines, clothes and beer. And everyone seems to speak English. The first time I "bought" a beer at the bar, three very stressed people immediately showed up, and in a very pedagogical and friendly way explained what *prix libre* means: you pay what you think something is worth or you pay what you can or have. The important thing isn't the price, but that you participate. But with that said, one of the people continued, explaining the price I had just paid for a beer was very high. "Are you calling me rich?" I asked, and he answered very apologetically, "Oh no, no, absolutely not!"

Everyone at Le Stendahl is so genuinely friendly that it warms my heart and strengthens my belief that a functioning anarchy doesn't really look quite the way people imagine.

- **A** 3 ave du Docteur Lannelongue, 92120 Montrouge
- **W** lestendhal.net

Point Éphémère 10 arr, concert venue
In this large, squat-like complex we saw the ferocious American band Ho99o9 less than ten

days after the attacks of November 13, 2015, which in a way felt heroic of everyone who was there, both on and in front of the stage.

Every other time, FMR (Ef-em-arr) has been very relaxed and fun. There are concerts nearly all the time, many of them good, and on weekends they serve brunch. In the summer you can take your plastic cups outside and settle down in the sun on the quayside where you can look at graffiti and watch the well-trained French firemen who jog past in large groups.

- **A** 200 Quai de Valmy, 75010 Paris
- **W** pointephemere.org
- **T** +33 1 40 34 02 48

Other good concert venues

La Mécanique Ondulatoire
- **A** 8 Passage Thiéré, 75011 Paris
- **W** mecanique-ondulatoire.com
- **T** +33 1 43 55 69 14

Instants Chavires
- **A** 7 rue Richard-Lenoir, 93100 Montreuil
- **T** +33 1 42 87 25 91

Musée Dupuytren
6 arr, museum
Musée Dupuytren is named after the surgeon who created this collection. His way is described as rare, reckless and striving, and he is best known for having given his name to the condition Dupuytren's contracture – or claw hand.

The museum is inside the university campus area, unmarked and forgotten among a lot of other buildings. The one little room is full of medical abnormalities and is extremely claustrophobic: only narrow corridors divided by glass display cases filled with animal and human body parts. It is also extremely interesting and merits some restraint and respect. Don't go here if you expect a laugh riot.

I think my favorite in the whole museum is the calf with two bodies. At first it feels like a worse version of the calf with two heads, but the longer you think about it, the stranger it gets.

Not for the faint of heart.

A 15 rue de l'École de Médecine, 75006 Paris
T +33 1 44 27 45 45

Herboristerie de la Place Clichy 8 arr, shop

An herbalist is a medicinal herb shop, but you don't actually have to go to a special herb store in Paris: all self-respecting pharmacies also sell herbal remedies. If you go to a pharmacy with a cold, often you'll leave with a packet full of both conventional medicine, something homeopathic and the pharmacy's own essential oils for the airways. But if you still want to visit a proper herbalist, this is the herbalist's herbalist – one of Europe's oldest. Plant parts are sold in bulk, over the counter, like at an old-fashioned general store; the staff are clad in white coats and are the littlest bit … special. But so skillful that there is often a line out the door.

A 87 rue d'Amsterdam, 75008 Paris
T +33 1 48 74 83 32

Monastica 4 arr, shop

I love everything in here. The handmade absinthe in wooden bottles, incense that you burn over glowing coals, beeswax candles, the rainbow-colored soaps that are made by monks, the essential oils and the unlimited amount of flower water. The shop is run by nuns and also sells things harvested and refined by the Cistercian order: a gang who thought the Franciscan order was altogether too lax and broke away to indulge in some really serious asceticism. For being one of the world's most unworldly groups, they are actually really good business people. Compared with the rest of the capitalist world they are, however, completely worthless. In here, a gentle monk can stand and stare horror-struck at the blipping card-reader thing, seemingly totally new to the concept of "credit cards". Thus, make sure you have a time buffer when you go here. You don't want to get into a situation where you're snapping at a nun. If you speak French it's fine to ask the nuns for advice: they know exactly which flower waters are good in cookies (lavender) and which essential oils go well with a little honey when sleep refuses to come and all you want is to feel like a clubbed seal (tropical basil).

A 10 rue des Barres, 75004 Paris
W monastica-art-et-artisanat.com
T +33 1 48 04 39 05

Marché aux Fleurs et aux Oiseaux 4 arr, market

This is the perfect outdoor market when you are on the hunt for an exotic palm, some potted lavender or a live rooster in a birdcage.

A allée Célestin Hennion, 75004 Paris

Vilmorin 1 arr, shop

Straight across the water from **Marché aux Fleurs et aux Oiseaux** (p. 171) are all of Paris' seed stores. Vilmorin is my favorite, but there's nothing wrong with the places that are next door to it, either.

A 6 Quai de la Mégisserie, 75001 Paris
W vilmorin-jardin.fr
T +33 1 42 33 61 62

⊙ 5 arr

Grande Mosquée de Paris
cafe and Turkish bathhouse

At Paris's largest mosque there's a nifty tea salon where people go to drink super sweet mint tea and eat Arabic baked goods filled with almond paste scented with rosewater. But the real secret is the Turkish bath, *Le Hamam*. In a corner of the tea salon stands a large cake counter set at an angle. Behind the counter – you have to lean to one side to pass by – there's an unmarked door. This is the door to the perfect excursion for those who like to travel without actually moving. Inside, is a church hall. The humidity feels like 100 percent, higher up in the cupola light sifts in through the colored-glass window, and everywhere – on the flagstones, at the fountain – naked women are sitting or lying.

The best time to go is at lunch, approximately between 1.30 and 2.30pm, when the bath is quietly abandoned. Around this time I lean my way in behind the cake counter and kick off my shoes. You pay 12 euro in the reception, which is so high it looks like a pulpit, and take a couple of bath slippers out of the communal basket. Continue to the changing room and change into a swimsuit. Go back out toward the church hall and then to the right, through yet another anonymous door marked only with the words "Bathing suits are obligatory in the hamam". This is the door to the restroom. I walk past the stalls with holes in the floor and continue to the restroom's far wall. There is yet another door. It leads to a fairly small room that is taken up almost entirely by two large white plastic bunks, of the type that I think are used in retirement homes. I continue to the next door which leads to a slightly bigger, warmer room. It's empty except for a garden hose on the floor and a stone bench filled with lots of sweaty women. I flop further in, through still another door and into the hamam's largest room. In the middle of the room is a low stone shelf, covered with mosaic in a design that looks both esoteric and mathematical. The ceiling, which was once totally blue, flakes in shades from sky blue to stormy gray. It wraps itself over small windows that let in a pinch of daylight. Along the walls are elevated stone alcoves with water taps and old plastic buckets with cut up plastic bottles in them. Here you can take a water bucket, slide down into a half-standing position, let your brain fog over again and only move when you must – to scoop more water over your head with the cut-up plastic bottles for example. Sometimes the water vapor is dispersed by a wind gust from the small network of vents. Look into a vent and it might be that a one-eyed pigeon stares back: the holes lead straight out to the fresh air. Everything at the hamam is provisional, glamorous, practical and decadent in a way that makes me think of Marianne Faithfull and Anita Pallenberg in Morocco.

Very farthest back in the large room is a last, dark doorway. The hamam's farthest room is small, dark and so hot that your nose-hairs sting. Inside in the dark there's a stairway that leads to a clear blue, illuminated, ice-cold pool, large enough for a person to plunge into, crouch under the water and then, gasping for breath, plunge back out again.

There is a rich and a poor way to go to the hamam (we could say luxurious and budget, but the hamam isn't really luxurious in that way).

In a complete spa bag I pack: water bottle, hand towel, swimsuit (or even better a bikini), at least 1 euro, plastic bag, *savon noir* (black soap), scrubbing glove, oil (argan oil is my favorite). The euro is to lock the locker, the water is so you don't faint, the plastic bag you need for wrangling the rest of your things. *Savon noir*, an ancient spa soap from Aleppo, is used this way: for at least 15 minutes you try to work as close to the warmest room as possible. Then you smear yourself with the soap and let it work for 5–10 minutes before you suds it up with strong, circular motions with the scrubbing mitten. Then you shower it

all off and finish with a dip in the ice-cold pool. After that you need a little emollient oil for the perfect Thousand and One Nights skin. All of these things – from the hamam's own *savon noir* to the scrub mittens – you can also buy or rent here.

Sometimes it's fun to treat yourself to a *gommage* (a professional scrub). You pay at the reception/pulpit and take with you a *gommage* amulet to the room with the retirement-home bunks in it. There, people sit in a line on a stone bench, while muscular Arab women scrub the skin of limp, rosy customers on the bunks in front of you. Once up on the plastic bunks, the best method is submission, with a pinch of psychic prophylaxis. When you wobble down from there, 5–10 rough minutes later, your shadow in 1:1 scale still lies on the bench, like a snake that shed its winter skin.

When it's time to squeeze back out past the cake counter, it's not just your skin that feels new – the whole city feels new.

Ⓐ 39 rue Saint-Hilaire, 75005 Paris
Ⓦ restaurantauxportesdelorient.com/hammam. html
Ⓣ +33 1 43 31 14 32

Jardin des Plantes 5 arr, garden
On the way to and from the mosque you pass Paris's botanical garden. Do not, for any reason in the world, miss the "corpse flower" as it's called in English. When it blooms usually there's a line along the street where it grows. If you aren't sure what it looks like, just follow the smell.

Ⓐ 57 rue Cuvier, 75005 Paris
Ⓦ jardindesplantes.net
Ⓣ +33 1 40 79 56 01

Index

Thanks to all our friends for having shared with us their favorite places.

À nos amis parisiens, d'où que vous venez. Merci pour les "saluts". Merci pour les shots. Merci d'avoir pris le temps de nous parler, même si nous étions seulement deux étrangers qui se présentaient à votre porte. Un grand merci de nous avoir fait découvrir votre ville, et damn you for making us miss you the rest of the time :) (and pardon our French).

Antoine, Rose et Emma; Medusa, Pierre, Louis et Antoine; Mike et Louis; Moro et David; Antoine et Sylvain; Geoff; Joe et Jen; Louise E.

Extra merci:
Thomas Klementsson, Guillaume Tomasi

Published in 2019 by ... is
a division of Hardie ... e
First published in 20 ... alia
Sweden
Original title: Paris f

Hardie Grant Travel
Building 1, 658 Chu
Richmond, Victoria

Hardie Grant Travel
Level 7, 45 Jones S
Ultimo, NSW 2007

www.hardiegrant.co

Copyright © Elin Ur
Copyright maps: © 2019 MAIRDUMONT,
D-73751 Ostfildern

Images page 134, 167 © Alamy

DATE DUE

PRINTED IN U.S.A.